MANCHESTER CITY F.C.

CITY OF CHAMPIONS

Legacy of Triumphs and Tribulations of Manchester City's Incredible Journey

By

O.A. Jackson

....

CONTENTS

....

Why this book?

The inspiration for this book dates back to the remarkable year of 2023 when Manchester City found themselves trailing Arsenal by a significant margin in the Premier League standings.

However, as fate would have it, the tides shifted, and City began a remarkable surge forward.

It was during this thrilling season that my 10-year-old grandson and I engaged in friendly football banter, a tradition we had upheld since the campaign's inception.

One particular conversation stands out in my memory. "Grandad, how do you think City will fare this season?" my grandson asked, with innocence and curiosity shining in his eyes. I must admit, as a lifelong supporter of the Red side of town, my loyalties were clear. Yet, I couldn't help but engage in the discussion.

"Not too well, hopefully. Maybe Arsenal will clinch the title," I playfully responded. Without a moment's hesitation, my cherished little Blue expressed unwavering confidence and pride, proclaiming, "We're going to win the Treble."

His bold statement took me aback. How could I respond to such conviction? Deep down, I acknowledged City's impressive run and its ability to overcome challenges in the past. Secretly, I knew they had a significant chance of securing the title.

However, I couldn't let him off the hook so easily. I couldn't just accept his confident prediction. Without hesitation, I proposed a wager. "Alright, if by some miracle City accomplishes the treble, which I highly doubt, I said. I will take you to the victory parade." To my surprise, he eagerly accepted, displaying the unwavering belief of a true fan.

As a birthday gift, I also wanted to provide him with something personal that would deepen his connection to his favorite team. I hope he enjoys it.
And so, this book came into existence. It serves as a chronicle of Manchester City's extraordinary journey during that unforgettable season, capturing the fulfillment of my promise to join my grandson at the victory parade, which, against all odds, became a reality.

As you delve into the pages that follow, you will witness the triumphs, the challenges, and the rollercoaster of emotions that unfolded, showcasing the power of belief and the unpredictable nature of football.

As we read through these pages you comprehend the challenges and the ups and down Manchester City had to go through to be where they are now. Therefore, this book was created from my grandson's viewpoint regarding his thoughts toward Manchester City. The illusive Treble was indeed won by City.

I went to the parade with him as I had promised. We watched as the player-filled bus passed us on Deansgate. I was overcome by the sense of pride that thousands of City supporters had produced. The fact that the rain did not stop.
Everyone who came to this momentous event was unaffected by it.

Get ready to hop into the pages of this book – it's like a cool tribute to all the ups and downs our Manchester City has seen.

This book spills the beans on how city transformed into the awesome team it is today.

Hold onto your hat, you're about to go on a wild ride of feelings, surprises popping up all over the place, and a story that mixes old memories with the amazing things happening right now.

This book takes you through their journey, the super exciting wins and the tough losses that tug at your heart.

By the end, you'll have this newfound love for how Manchester City has grown and changed.

So, all you City fans, get ready to jump into this literary adventure where the past and present shake hands like old pals.

It's your chance to relive those sweet memories from back in the day while giving a high-five to the team's current victories.

Embrace the mystery and enjoy every moment.

Enjoy.

PART 1

Introduction

Unveiling Manchester City's Legendary Journey

Step right into the exhilarating world of Manchester City Football Club, a pulsating pilgrimage through time awaits, stirring emotions that transcend mere sport. The journey unfolds with a burst of energy, weaving threads of triumph, resilience, and unwavering loyalty that bind us to this beloved club.

From its humble origins, the rise to prominence is celebrated, transforming Manchester City into an unstoppable force. Visionary managers and mesmerizing talents collide in a symphony of skill, crafting a team destined for football glory, etching our name in history.

Yet, in the whirlwind of triumph, challenges abound, testing our mettle to the core. We weather storms that threaten to dampen our spirit, but hope prevails, forging an unbreakable bond in the fiery depths of the sky blue spirit.

Glory descends like magic, as Manchester City graces the stages of domestic and European football, the taste of victory lingering on our tongues. Unforgettable matches leave us breathless, hearts pounding in ecstasy.

But the journey of a true fan brims with intensity, navigating rough waters and standing tall amidst controversies, unwavering in loyalty. Defining moments unite us as one, defending the honor of our beloved club with heads held high.

Under new leadership, the renaissance emerges, as Manchester City reinvents itself, embracing a new identity. The modern era knows no limits, breaking records and soaring to heights beyond imagination.

In the tapestry of this remarkable journey, legendary players adorn the sacred sky blue jersey, etching their names in the hearts of fans worldwide. Their audacious skills and brilliance immortalize them in the annals of Manchester City's hallowed history.

The enduring spirit of Manchester City defies logic, transcending boundaries, igniting passion across the globe. From local streets to the global stage, the tale of this beloved club is a testament to unwavering loyalty, a bond that unites us all.

So, dive into these pages and brace yourself for an enigmatic adventure. Embrace the surge of adrenaline, savor the joy, and embrace the pain of being a true Sky Blue. Together, let's celebrate the history, triumphs, and unyielding passion that make Manchester City Football Club more than a team, but a way of life.

Ready to be mesmerized?

Let's go!

··

PART 2

To St. Mark's Church in Gorton and beyond

··

From 1880

Welcome to the enigmatic world of Manchester City F.C., a club with roots intertwined with St. Mark's Church in Gorton, Manchester, during its formative years from 1880 to 1887. The details of our origins remain shrouded in mystery, but the efforts of the church and key individuals like Arthur Connell, Anna Connell, William Beastow, Thomas Goodbehere, and James Moores paved the path for our existence.

In those early days, Gorton grappled with social challenges, its young men caught in street fights. In response, the church sought to redirect their energy to more constructive activities, forming a young men's association and even a cricket team during the summer months.

Football soon crept into the picture, and St. Mark's recorded their first match against a church team from Macclesfield on November 13, 1880. They faced struggles initially but celebrated their first victory over Stalybridge Clarence in March 1881.

The involvement of Anna Connell in the football team's formation remains a subject of speculation. While some believe she played a pivotal role, official historians dispute this, acknowledging her contributions to men's meetings and activities but lacking concrete evidence linking her to the team.

Amidst the changes and mergers, St. Mark's title waned, and Gorton Association F.C. began to embrace its identity independently, with a symbol adorning their shirts – a black strip and a white cross pattée.

Cup competitions brought moments of elation and disappointment. In 1886, Gorton Association triumphed over West Gorton Athletic with a 5-1 victory but faced a crushing defeat against Newton Heath in the Second Round, a resounding 11-1 loss. Nonetheless, the club's cup success was on the horizon.

Our roots in St. Mark's Church and the endeavors of Arthur Connell, William Beastow, Thomas Goodbehere, and others laid the foundation for Manchester City's early development. The journey from St. Mark's to Gorton Association marked the beginning of a storied history.
The Majestic Manchester City Squad that Seized the FA Cup in 1904.
Being the first club to win a major cup by beating Bolton Wanderers 1 – 0 in the final
Glory Ignited:

However, obstacles lurked ahead, with allegations of financial irregularities and a suspension of seventeen players, including our esteemed captain, Billy Meredith, in 1906. It was a trying time, but the spirit of Manchester City endured, unbroken in the face of adversity.

We rose from the ashes like the mighty phoenix, fueled by our undying love for the club. In 1920, a devastating fire engulfed the main stand at Hyde

Road, a place where we shared countless memories. But even this couldn't stop us. In 1923, we embraced a new chapter, moving to our purpose-built fortress at Maine Road in Moss Side. It became a symbol of our resilience and determination, a home that echoed with the roars of our loyal supporters.

Let me tell you about Maine Road

This was a timeless football fortress in the heart of Manchester. From 1923 to 2003, this hallowed ground embraced the spirit of Manchester City F.C., witnessing glorious victories and inspiring the hearts of devoted fans.

The last match at Maine Road. The match with a 0 – 1 defeat by Southampton.
Just to rub salt into the wounds. Michael Svensson scored the goal.

It stood proud as the backdrop for the FA Cup semi-finals, the prestigious Charity Shield, the exhilarating League Cup finals, and even unforgettable clashes of national pride.

PART 3
YEARS - 1928 – 1965

Hold on tight as we dive into the passionate whirlwind of Manchester City's iconic history. The 1930s unfurled with true mettle, propelling us to two consecutive FA Cup finals. Though Everton bested us in 1933, our triumphant roar echoed in 1934, seizing the coveted Cup by defeating Portsmouth.

Amidst that epic cup run, history was etched. A colossal sea of 84,569 fervent fans flooded Maine Road. An English football attendance record that stands undefeated. Electric vibes pulsated as we faced Stoke City in the sixth round FA Cup tie of 1934 - a sight to behold, a testament to our unwavering fanbase's undying support.

But the glory didn't halt there. In 1937, we carved our name into the annals of football greatness, seizing the First Division title for the first time. We reveled in the apex of English football, basking in the brilliance of our achievement.. Fate wove a cruel twist. The subsequent season found us relegated, despite outscoring all others in the division. A bitter blow, yet it couldn't quench our fighting spirit.

Fast forward twenty years, a new generation of City heroes arose, ignited by the tactical brilliance of the Revie Plan. (Manchester City used the Revie Plan as a tactical system in association football in the 1950s. The method was named after Manchester City player Don Revie, who played a key part in its development.

The Hungarian national team shocked English football in 1953, beating England 6-3 at Wembley Stadium. The Revie plan was an adaptation on the Hungarian tactics, with Don Revie playing as a deep-lying centre-forward, similar to Hungarian striker Nándor Hidegkuti. Revie started attacks by coming into the middle of the field to receive the ball, forcing the opposing center-half into a defensive position. The function can be connected to the present false 9 role).

It was a golden era that witnessed us, once again, soar to consecutive FA Cup finals in 1955 and 1956. The first, against Newcastle United, wasn't in our favour, but that didn't deter us. In 1956, we stormed back with vengeance, triumphing over Birmingham City in a historic final.

That final, etched in our memories forever. A 3-1 victory that still reverberates in celebration. But what rendered it truly legendary was the indomitable spirit of our goalkeeper, Bert Trautmann. Unbeknownst to him, he played on, breaking his neck during the game, yet showcasing unrivaled determination and love for the club. A heroic act, encapsulating the resilience and spirit of Manchester City.

These moments define us as City fans. Triumphs and heartbreaks interweave, but through it all, our passion blazes brighter. We carry the legacy of our predecessors, honoring their contributions, cherishing the very spirit that makes Manchester City so extraordinary. As we stride forth on this incredible journey, we do so with unwavering belief and an unbreakable bond.
We are the Citizens, and together, we rise!

PART 4

YEARS - 1965 – 2001

What a rollercoaster ride it's been, my fellow passionate Manchester City fans! The 1960s served up defining moments that tested our spirit and resilience.

After a gut-wrenching relegation to the Second Division in 1963, our beloved club plummeted to rock bottom, witnessing a record-low attendance. The horizon appeared gloomy, but little did we know that a dawn of change was lurking.

Enter the saviors of summer 1965, Joe Mercer and Malcolm Allison. With their visionary guidance, a metamorphosis commenced. Under Mercer's leadership, we soared victoriously, seizing the Second Division title in our very first season. The acquisitions of legends like Mike Summerbee and Colin Bell breathed new life into the team, igniting a spark of hope and dreams.

Then arrived the glorious 1967-68 season, etched in golden letters across Manchester City's history. On that fateful final day, hearts pounded wildly as we clinched the League Championship in a nerve-wracking 4-3 victory against Newcastle United. The ecstasy of knowing we had triumphed over our arch-rivals, Manchester United, to seize the ultimate prize.

Trophies flowed in, each adding to our illustrious legacy. In 1969, the FA Cup was secured, followed by European glory in 1970 with the lifting of the European Cup Winners' Cup in Vienna. The energy of that night was electric, as we conquered

Górnik Zabrze, forever etching our name in footballing annals. But we weren't done yet. The League Cup was added to our haul that very season, making us only the second English team to seize a European trophy and a domestic one in a single campaign.

The 1970s witnessed continued battles for honors, coming achingly close to league glory on two occasions. But one match, oh, one match still sends shivers down our spines. The 1973-74 season's final game against arch-rivals Manchester United, a moment of immense significance. Former United player Denis Law, the hero in our midst, delivered a backheel goal, sealing their relegation and igniting our jubilation.

That moment epitomizes the passion and rivalry of Manchester football, eternally etched in our hearts.

Our quest for success persisted, triumphing in the 1976 League Cup final against Newcastle United. A sweet victory, a testament to the unwavering determination of our team.

At Wembley, in a thrilling encounter against Newcastle United, Manchester City emerged triumphant with a 2-1 scoreline, clinching their second League Cup title.

An 11th-minute strike from the youthful brilliance of 19-year-old Peter Barnes set the stage, his powerful shot eluding the outstretched arms of Newcastle's goalkeeper, Mike Mahoney.

Resilient Newcastle equalized after 35 minutes through Alan Gowling, courtesy of Malcolm MacDonald's deft assist.

The first half concluded with a golden chance for City, but Mahoney's remarkable save denied Dennis Tueart.

In the 46th minute, a precise cross from Willie Donachie met Tommy Booth's well-directed header at the back post, restoring City's lead. The thrill of victory surged within us, as the legend of Manchester City continued to flourish, forever etched in the sands of time.

With his back to the net, Tueart instinctively executed a breathtaking bicycle kick, directing the ball into the bottom corner beyond Mahoney's reach.

This extraordinary goal etched itself into the annals of Manchester City's history, becoming one of their most celebrated moments.

The Team's 1976 League Cup Final. Final Score 2 - 1
City: Corrigan, Keegan, Donachie, Doyle (c), Watson, Oakes, Barnes, Booth, Royle, Hartford, Tueart

Sub: Clements

Newcastle: Mahoney, Nattrass, Kennedy, Keeley, Howard, Barrowclough, Cassidy, Craig (c), Burns, MacDonald, Gowling

Sub: Cannell

The drama unfolded as both teams relentlessly battled to alter the scoreline, but City's defense held its ground, ensuring victory and clinching the League Cup for the second time. A momentous achievement for Tony Book, becoming the first individual to conquer the competition as both player and manager, magnifying City's success on this unforgettable occasion.

A period of decline loomed ahead.

The 1980s descended upon us with a tumult of managerial changes and struggles. Malcolm Allison's return as manager brought squandered funds on unsuccessful signings. Relegation battles and bittersweet cup finals, like the elusive 1981 FA Cup final against Tottenham Hotspur, tested our resilience. The 1990s offered fleeting respite under Peter Reid's guidance, with fifth-place league finishes. Yet, our momentary success gave way to turbulent tides once more.

We co-founded the Premier League in 1992, but our fortunes faded. Despite a valiant ninth-place finish in the inaugural season, we plummeted into a three-year struggle, culminating in relegation in 1996. Our hearts sank, plummeting to the depths of Division One. Oh, the anguish endured as we became the second-ever European trophy winners relegated to the third tier of English football.

Our tale breathes resilience, rebirth, and unwavering support. Challenges fortify our love for the club. From the ashes, we rise, prepared to conquer new heights and create more enchanting moments that shall echo through eternity.

PART 5

2001 – Present

Then up & up

But hey, City never backs down! We co-founded the Premier League in 1992, but we had our fair share of struggles. Relegation in 1996 hit us hard, sending us to the third tier, an unimaginable fate for a European trophy winner.

But we are resilient, we are Cityzens! Guided by David Bernstein, we embraced a new era of financial responsibility, fighting our way back to the top flight. The playoff victory against Gillingham reignited our fire, and we returned to the Premier League with Kevin Keegan's inspirational leadership, securing the Division One championship in 2001-02.

Our journey continued, marked by unforgettable moments. Victory over Manchester United in the derby, breaking a 13-year wait, shook the footballing world. European competition beckoned after a quarter-century, and the City of Manchester Stadium became our fortress.

New faces, new hope, and the Abu Dhabi United Group's takeover transformed us into a force to be reckoned with. Shattering transfer records, welcoming stars like Robinho, Carlos Tevez, and Emmanuel Adebayor, City announced its ambition.

Under Roberto Mancini, we achieved domestic glory, securing an unprecedented domestic treble. We celebrated, breaking records and captivating fans worldwide.

We faced adversity, but we never faltered. UEFA's ban threatened our ambitions, but we fought back, and justice prevailed. Our commitment to fair play and determination to succeed saw the ban overturned.
Under Pep Guardiola, we reached new heights. League titles reclaimed, records broken, and the Champions League final within grasp. Though victory eluded us, our journey showcased the strength of Manchester City.

And now, Erling Haaland joins our ranks, a symbol of our ambition. With renewed hope and determination, we aim to etch our name in history. Our treble-winning campaign proves our unwavering belief and unity.

Manchester City, the heartbeat of a city, the pride of a nation. Passionate souls bleeding blue, carrying the torch through thick and thin. We forge a legacy that echoes through eternity.
Together, we rise, conquer, and paint the world sky-blue. City forever!

PART - 6

What Now ?

Reflections and going forward

As a fervent Manchester City supporter, reminiscing on the club's journey fills me with an overwhelming mix of pride and joy. It hasn't been all smooth sailing, oh no, but those ups and downs, they've added that extra sprinkle of meaning to our accomplishments.

From the gut-wrenching days of relegation to the soaring heights of domestic and international glory, Manchester City's transformation is a dazzling display of unwavering spirit, both from the club and its fiercely devoted supporters.

I still vividly recall those dark, tumultuous times when financial turmoil threatened to eclipse our light. The winds of change swept in with new ownership and the visionary leadership of the likes of Sheikh Mansour. Financial resources poured in, and oh, did we ever attract world-class talent, building a squad that was nothing short of formidable. Trophies were beckoning, and our dreams seemed within reach.

Let's not forget the magic conjured on the pitch under the stewardship of mesmerizing managers like Roberto Mancini, Manuel Pellegrini, and Pep Guardiola. The style of play was simply jaw-dropping, breathtaking, attacking football that bewitched fans worldwide. The intricate passing, the sheer dominance on that hallowed ground—it made us a force to be reckoned with, and how!

Speaking of silverware, we've stacked up quite the collection in recent years. Premier League titles, FA Cups, League Cups. We even set our sights on that elusive Champions League trophy! Record-breaking, history-making, Manchester City has emerged as the epitome of excellence in the grand theater of football.

It's not just the glittering trophies that set us apart. It's the unrivaled passion and loyalty of the fans, the unwavering support that paints Manchester City's true colors. Come rain or shine, in victory or defeat, we have stood tall, singing our hearts out, turning the Etihad Stadium into a cauldron of passion and energy. We've formed an unbreakable bond with the players, the staff, and one another.

The future, it's bursting with excitement and optimism for Manchester City. The arrival of Erling Haaland is the clarion call of our intent to keep challenging for honours, to stand firm among the elite. The hunger for success courses through our veins, and with Pep Guardiola at the helm, greatness is etched in our destiny.

Onward we march, but let us not forget our core values and the sense of unity that defines us. As passionate fans, we must continue our unwavering support, raising the roof and creating an intimidating fortress for our adversaries. Our collective passion is the spark that ignites the players, driving them to scale new heights and claim even grander triumphs.

Nurturing the young talents from our esteemed academy—that's the key to the club's long-term prosperity. Our hearts swell with pride as local talents rise through the ranks and represent the sky-blue colors on the grandest stages. Let's foster youth development and keep our identity alive, lighting the path for a bright, dazzling future for Manchester City.

Moreover, as a club deeply rooted in the embrace of Manchester's community, let's give back, let's make a difference. Engaging in charitable endeavors, supporting local causes, being a beacon of positivity within the city's heart—these deeds will weave an unbreakable bond between us and the community, making us more than just a football club.
Of course, challenges will always rear their heads on this never-ending football journey. But with the fervor, the resilience, and the rock-solid support of the fans, Manchester City will not just survive but thrive. Together, we shall build a legacy that future generations will inherit with boundless pride.

As a passionate Manchester City fan, my heart is ablaze with hope, brimming with anticipation for the adventures ahead. The journey is far from over, and I am eagerly awaiting the continued success, the captivating football, and the unwavering spirit that make our beloved club so extraordinary. Let the sky-blue flag flutter high, and may we march forth together, singing in unison for the grandeur of Manchester City!

PART 7

The Funnier Side

Did they really say and do that?

Brace yourself for a delightful burst of perplexing anecdotes related to the illustrious Manchester City FC! Hold on tight as we embark on a whirlwind tour of tales involving players, managers, and reporters alike:

Roberto Mancini, the mastermind manager, once donned a sneaky disguise, transforming into a pizza delivery man to surprise the players with late-night treats after a sweet victory!

Vincent Kompany, the esteemed former captain, humbled himself by cleaning his boots in the dressing room—his secret to staying grounded amidst fame and success.

Oh, the remorseful Sergio Aguero! After a missed penalty, he gallantly paid for the fans' drinks at a local pub as a heartfelt apology.
Pep Guardiola, the meticulous strategist, took perfectionism to another level, rearranging training ground cones until they met his impeccable standards, much to the amusement of the players.

Ah, the charm of David Silva! Our beloved player carried a lucky stone in his socks during matches, believing it brought him all the good fortune.

Mario Balotelli, the mercurial talent, once set his house ablaze with fireworks, summoning the fire brigade for an unexpected rendezvous.

Yaya Toure, the midfield maestro, unexpectedly interrupted a post-match interview, personally thanking a journalist for their favorable coverage—now, that's gratitude!

Passionate Pep's fiery halftime talks—memorable, yes, but beware the broken whiteboard during one particularly intense speech that startled the players!

The stuff of legends! The Premier League title secured by Sergio Aguero's last-minute goal, immortalized by Martin Tyler's iconic cry of "Agueroooo!"

Joe Hart, the charismatic goalkeeper, stumbled upon an elderly supporter while grocery shopping and spent hours chatting—oh, the power of chance encounters!

Kevin De Bruyne, the midfield wizard, had childhood dreams of being Michael Owen, even imitating his goal celebrations during backyard matches.

The unshakable calm of Manuel Pellegrini, the former manager, remained undeterred even during a post-match interview swarmed by bees—bees, yes!

Pep Guardiola's time-keeping eccentricity—when he arrived, all clocks at the training ground were set five minutes ahead, ensuring punctuality galore!

Fernandinho, the thoughtful Brazilian, orchestrated a surprise birthday bash for Pep, expressing gratitude for the manager's impact on the team.

Comical Pep! In the midst of a press conference, he playfully interrupted a reporter mid-question, urging him to chill and relax because nerves, ah, nerves!

Kyle Walker, the right-back with a heart of gold, warmed hearts when he graced a young fan's birthday party after seeing him dress up as his hero for Halloween.

Richard Dunne, the former captain, once faced a half-time conundrum, accidentally locking himself in the toilet—oh, the dramatic delay!

The appreciative Raheem Sterling! He treated the employees of a convenience store to ice cream as a token of gratitude for their unwavering support.

Pep Guardiola's unmatched fashion sense! Spotted donning stylish outfits on the sidelines, he topped it off by gifting personalized bathrobes to the players, a dash of elegance

These stories highlight the endearing camaraderie and enjoyable times at Manchester City FC, as players, managers, and supporters come together in the captivating game of football!

So there you have it—a flurry of 20 stories that lift the lid and shed light on the more humorous aspects of Manchester City FC's journey—a roller coaster of feelings, victories, and charming eccentricities that characterize our beloved team!

PART 8

Ups & Downs

132 years of ups and down but the end was worth the wait

Embarking on a captivating odyssey through the annals of time, we delve into Manchester City's prodigious history, spanning from their nascent inception in 1892 to the illustrious year of 2021. Brace yourself for an enigmatic voyage, as we navigate through the labyrinthine web of divisions and positions that have defined the club's remarkable journey in the realm of football.

Glimpse back to the inception of Manchester City in the 1890s, where they gallantly emerged in the Second Division, seizing the runner-up position with unwavering determination. A triumphant surge followed, as they ascended to the top, clinching the pinnacle position and gloriously attaining promotion to the revered First Division.

The subsequent years brought forth a mesmerizing tapestry of outcomes, replete with undulating fortunes and beguiling complexities. Their mercurial voyage through the First Division showcased an array of placements, flitting between the enchanting realms of 6th, 9th, 10th, and 12th positions. The emotions accompanied Manchester City's trajectory, experiencing both the exultation of lofty standings and the introspection demanded by more modest ranks. The annals bore witness to their tenure amidst the 15th and 16th positions, each season unveiling novel challenges and enigmatic twists.

Experiencing the ebb and flow of fate, Manchester City thrived in the First Division, capturing the apex with unparalleled flair in the 1901-1902 season, adorned as the Champions. Such awe-inspiring supremacy was met with subsequent oscillations, settling in at 6th and 3rd positions.

The enthralling drama continued to unfold, oscillating from the heights of 2nd place to the tranquil embrace of 4th and 5th. Peaks and troughs of brilliance sculpted their journey, culminating in the crowning glory of consecutive championships in the 1911-1912 and 1912-1913 seasons, exultantly entwined in the annals of history.

Yet, the labyrinthine course of time brought forth trials and tribulations, encountering the tempestuous climes of the 15th position, a momentary nadir amidst their illustrious narrative. Embarking on an eventful hiatus during the First World War, their indomitable spirit persevered, heralding a phoenix-like resurgence.

Resuming their voyage, Manchester City grappled with unforeseen adversities, savoring sweet promotions, and navigating the shadows of relegation. As the pages unfurled, their unwavering tenacity propelled them to seize the 21st and 22nd positions, engaging in the delicate ballet between ascension and descent.

The passage of time witnessed a symphony of fluctuations, embellished with triumphant conquests and introspective evaluations. A momentous promotion to the Second Division embellished their legacy, while periods of lucid brilliance were juxtaposed with earnest struggles in the 14th and 21st positions.

A crescendo of destiny awaited them in the Third Division North, as they mounted the pinnacle of triumph, savoring the crown of champions. The ethereal jubilation reverberated through the corridors of time, invigorating their spirit as they surged forth.

The irresistible tides of history ushered them back to the Second Division, where they engaged in a dance with destiny, ascending to 2nd place, ascending once more to the hallowed First Division, greeted with renewed vigor and hope.

Adventuring through the mid-20th century, Manchester City enthralled audiences with an alluring tapestry of endeavors. Amidst the vibrant vibrato of the First Division, they traversed diverse positions, cascading between 18th, 7th, and 11th, each a testament to the enigmatic allure of football.

The 1960s heralded a symphony of resplendent achievements, capturing hearts and minds with successive championships in the 1965-1966, 1967-1968, and 1968-1969 seasons, earning the title of Champions with unassailable prowess.

As the pendulum of time swung, Manchester City navigated the undulating landscapes of the First Division, their positions ranging from 13th to 4th, oscillating with verve and vitality.
The waning years of the century unfurled a bittersweet reverie, characterized by fervent struggles, relegations, and triumphant promotions.

The dawn of a new millennium brought with it fresh aspirations and renewed determination. Manchester City scaled the dazzling echelons of the Premier League, reveling in the splendor of 9th, 16th, and 8th positions, illuminating the footballing firmament with their brilliance.

Yet, the crescendo of destiny awaited them in the 2011-2012 season, etching an indelible chapter in football history. In an unforgettable climax, Manchester City soared to the top, securing the coveted crown of Champions, entwined in the throes of an epic battle with rivals, leaving fans awestruck.

The enthralling tale continues, interweaving fluctuations of fate and tempestuous turns. The mystique of Manchester City's journey is enigmatic, captivating our senses as we traverse through the maze of their footballing legacy.

Thus, their saga unfolds, an intricate tapestry, ever-entwined with the grand symphony of football's allure, leaving us enraptured by the enigmatic spell cast by Manchester City, a club that transcends the realms of time and space, forever imprinted in the annals of sporting legendry.

Here is the list of all the divisions and places Manchester City ended in each season since the start, from 1892 to 2021, in a single column:

1892-1893: Second Division - 2nd place
1893-1894: Second Division - 1st place (promoted to First Division)
1894-1895: First Division - 6th place
1895-1896: First Division - 9th place
1896-1897: First Division - 10th place
1897-1898: First Division - 12th place

1898-1899: First Division - 15th place

1899-1900: First Division - 16th place

1900-1901: First Division - 10th place

1901-1902: First Division - 1st place (Champions)

1902-1903: First Division - 6th place

1903-1904: First Division - 1st place (Champions)

1904-1905: First Division - 3rd place

1905-1906: First Division - 2nd place

1906-1907: First Division - 4th place

1907-1908: First Division - 4th place

1908-1909: First Division - 2nd place

1909-1910: First Division - 5th place

1910-1911: First Division - 2nd place

1911-1912: First Division - 1st place (Champions)

1912-1913: First Division - 1st place (Champions)

1913-1914: First Division - 15th place

1914-1915: First Division - 5th place

1915-1919: League suspended due to World War I

1919-1920: First Division - 7th place

1920-1921: First Division - 6th place

1921-1922: First Division - 15th place

1922-1923: First Division - 21st place (relegated to Second Division)

1923-1924: Second Division - 7th place

1924-1925: Second Division - 10th place

1925-1926: Second Division - 3rd place

1926-1927: Second Division - 5th place

1927-1928: Second Division - 3rd place

1928-1929: Second Division - 2nd place (promoted to First Division)

1929-1930: First Division - 14th place

1930-1931: First Division - 21st place (relegated to Second Division)

1931-1932: Second Division - 8th place

1932-1933: Second Division - 21st place (relegated to Third Division North)

1933-1934: Third Division North - 2nd place (promoted to Second Division)

1934-1935: Second Division - 22nd place (relegated to Third Division North)

1935-1936: Third Division North - 10th place

1936-1937: Third Division North - 1st place (promoted to Second Division)

1937-1938: Second Division - 22nd place (relegated to Third Division North)

1938-1939: Third Division North - 1st place (promoted to Second Division)

2ND WORLD WAR INTERVENES

1946-1947: Second Division - 19th place

1947-1948: Second Division - 19th place

1948-1949: Second Division - 19th place

1949-1950: Second Division - 3rd place

1950-1951: Second Division - 5th place

1951-1952: First Division - 18th place

1952-1953: First Division - 18th place

1953-1954: First Division - 7th place

1954-1955: First Division - 11th place

1955-1956: First Division - 1st place (Champions)

1956-1957: First Division - 2nd place

1957-1958: First Division - 5th place

1958-1959: First Division - 3rd place

1959-1960: First Division - 2nd place

1960-1961: First Division - 4th place

1961-1962: First Division - 4th place

1962-1963: First Division - 8th place

1963-1964: First Division - 7th place

1964-1965: First Division - 2nd place

1965-1966: First Division - 15th place

1966-1967: First Division - 1st place (Champions)

1967-1968: First Division - 1st place (Champions)

1968-1969: First Division - 7th place

1969-1970: First Division - 13th place

1970-1971: First Division - 11th place

1971-1972: First Division - 4th place

1972-1973: First Division - 11th place

1973-1974: First Division - 2nd place

1974-1975: First Division - 15th place

1975-1976: First Division - 8th place

1976-1977: First Division - 15th place

1977-1978: First Division - 11th place

1978-1979: Second Division - 20th place (relegated to Third Division)

1979-1980: Third Division - 21st place (relegated to Fourth Division)

1980-1981: Fourth Division - 8th place

1981-1982: Fourth Division - 20th place

1982-1983: Fourth Division - 21st place

1983-1984: Fourth Division - 3rd place (promoted to Third Division)

1984-1985: Third Division - 4th place

1985-1986: Third Division - 7th place

1986-1987: Third Division - 5th place

1987-1988: Third Division - 6th place

1988-1989: Third Division - 5th place

1989-1990: Third Division - 14th place

1990-1991: Third Division - 5th place

1991-1992: Third Division - 1st place (promoted to Second Division)

1992-1993: Second Division - 9th place

1993-1994: First Division - 16th place

1994-1995: Premier League - 17th place

1995-1996: Premier League - 18th place (relegated to First Division)

1996-1997: First Division - 14th place

1997-1998: First Division - 22nd place (relegated to Second Division)

1998-1999: Second Division - 3rd place

1999-2000: Second Division - 2nd place (promoted to First Division)

2000-2001: First Division - 3rd place

2001-2002: Premier League - 9th place

2002-2003: Premier League - 9th place

2003-2004: Premier League - 16th place

2004-2005: Premier League - 8th place

2005-2006: Premier League - 15th place

2006-2007: Premier League - 14th place

2007-2008: Premier League - 9th place

2008-2009: Premier League - 10th place

2009-2010: Premier League - 5th place

2010-2011: Premier League - 3rd place

2011-2012: Premier League - 1st place (Champions)

In one of the most unforgettable endings to a league season, Manchester City clinched their first Premier League title, joining an elite group of champions. Finishing level on 89 points with rivals Manchester United, City's superior goal difference, eight goals better, secured their historic triumph. This remarkable feat showcased their unwavering determination and marked a watershed moment in their history, solidifying their status among football's greats. The thrilling conclusion epitomized the captivating drama of the sport, forever etching City's name in the annals of footballing glory.

2012-2013: Premier League - 2nd place

2013-2014: Premier League - 1st place (Champions)

Liverpool's long-awaited Premier League title seemed within their grasp, but Manchester City had other plans. Through a combination of favorable outcomes and unwavering consistency, City secured their second league championship in just three years, thwarting Liverpool's hopes of lifting the trophy.

2014-2015: Premier League - 2nd place

2015-2016: Premier League - 4th place

2016-2017: Premier League - 3rd place

2017-2018: Premier League - 1st place (Champions)

Pep Guardiola's Manchester City showcased an incredibly dominant campaign, arguably one of the most dominant in Premier League history. From the very start, they exuded an aura of invincibility, aiming to shatter the record for the most points in a season. Led by the outstanding performances of Raheem Sterling and Kevin De Bruyne, City reigned supreme, securing the Premier League title once more and etching their name among the illustrious list of previous winners.

2018-2019: Premier League - 1st place (Champions)

In a captivating battle between Liverpool and Manchester City, it was the latter who emerged victorious, claiming the top spot with an impressive 98 points. Liverpool fought valiantly, fiercely challenging for the title and intermittently occupying the coveted position, but ultimately settled for an incredibly close second with 97 points. Chelsea secured a distant third place with 72 points, while Tottenham and Arsenal followed in fourth and fifth places respectively. The race for the Premier League crown was a thrilling spectacle, showcasing the intense competition among these top teams.

2019-2020: Premier League - 2nd place

2020-2021: Premier League - 1st place (Champions)

Manchester City dominated the 29th season of the Premier League, emphatically claiming their fifth Premier League title and seventh English league title in total. Their triumph came with an impressive three matches remaining, showcasing their exceptional form and superiority throughout the campaign. This victory also marked City's third league title in the last four seasons, solidifying their status as a force to be reckoned with in English football.

2021-2022: Premier League - 1st place (Champions)

The final day of the 2022 Premier League season unfolded as a thrilling two-horse race between Manchester City and Liverpool. However, it was Manchester City who delivered an extraordinary spectacle, orchestrating a remarkable comeback to defeat Aston Villa 3-2 and secure the title with an impressive tally of 93 points. Liverpool finished agonizingly close, falling short by just a single point, while Chelsea settled for a distant third place with 74 points. The dramatic climax to the season showcased the sheer intensity and unpredictability of the Premier League, leaving fans in awe of the incredible displays of skill and determination from the top contenders.

2022-2023: Premier League - 1st place (Champions)

Despite a strong performance throughout the season, Arsenal's aspirations of securing their first title in years were dashed as the unstoppable

Manchester City continued their dominant reign, clinching their fifth Premier League title in six years. This remarkable achievement places City in an elite category, with only Manchester United having matched this record from the 1995/96 to 2000/01 seasons. Arsenal's valiant efforts fell short in the face of City's relentless form, underscoring the immense challenge posed by the reigning champions and their unparalleled consistency in recent years.

Note: The list includes both promotions and relegations throughout Manchester City's history.

PART 9

The Legends

Notable managers and players from Manchester City FC's history

As we enter the hallowed halls of Manchester City's legendary legacy, we find ourselves surrounded by a constellation of players and managers, similar to attempting to count the infinite stars that adorn the nocturnal canvas or counting the innumerable renditions of "Blue Moon" serenading the Etihad Stadium.

Indeed, a daring attempt that pushes the frontiers of possible! Undaunted, we will embark on this journey, traversing the maze of personal opinion as we seek for the actual luminaries who have engraved their names in the annals of this organization.

With bated breath, we could endlessly repeat a never-ending roster of players and managers, only to realize that the regions of excellence are, in fact, subjective territories. As the age-old discussion about the color of the sky and the verdancy of the grass continues, so does the subjectivity of football's legends, who tempt us with their thoughts.

Rest assured, City enthusiasts! We have mustered the courage to name the individuals who have unquestionably contributed to the glorious fabric of this club's history. We moved ahead, relying on our instincts and the furnace of history, despite the lack of a crystal ball or spectral guidance from bygone City legends.

Raise your chalices in honor of those who have left us an everlasting tapestry of unforgettable moments, throbbing victories, and awe-inspiring goals. Cheers to the revered individuals that graced the sacred pitch with their ethereal brilliance, ardent ardour, and a touch of mysticism. And let us remember the famous tacticians, the helmsmen who guided our ship through stormy waters and established a course to victory.

Whether it be the iconic Colin Bell, the mesmerising Mike Summerbee, the enigmatic Sergio Aguero, or the illustrious Pep Guardiola, each wove their magic into the fabric of this club, eliciting delirious joy, ecstatic tears, and, on rare occasions, the flinging of remote controls across the room in exasperation.

Let us celebrate football's symphony, delight in the sheer euphoria it inspires, and glorify the giants who have engraved Manchester City's very soul. In the end, it is not just about the players and managers that graced the stage, but also about us, the ardent fans who have stood by the club through the whims of fate, through tempests and triumphs, and, yes, even those perplexing "WTF" moments.

So, let the voices of everyone soar, melodiously shouting the anthem of our devotion, and let us all rejoice in unison for our dear Manchester City. For we are woven together into this mesmerizing narrative, and perhaps in the days ahead, we will celebrate new symbols added to the fabric of stories. That's fantastic!

And now, let us glance upon the intrepid helmsmen who steered Manchester City's course through the tides of history:

Managers

Joe Mercer (1965-1971): A maestro of his time, guiding the team to their first league title in 44 years during the 1967-68 season.

Roberto Mancini (2009-2013), a virtuoso of the tactical arts, unveiled a symphony of stratagems that culminated in Manchester City's maiden Premier League triumph in the 2011-2012 season. A visionary conductor, he orchestrated a melodic crescendo, wherein the echoes of victory resonated through the very foundations of the club.

In the epoch of Pep Guardiola (2016-present), the footballing firmament bore witness to a savant whose genius surpassed the realms of comprehension. Illuminating Manchester City, he adorned the club with multiple league titles and domestic cup glories, a meteor shower of achievements that dazzled the world.

Enter Malcolm Allison (1972-1980), a luminary imbued with acumen so profound that his influence echoed through the corridors of time. An alchemist of management, his dual roles as assistant manager and manager forged an indelible mark upon the team's success, an enigmatic legacy that defies explication.

Venture into the saga of Manuel Pellegrini (2013-2016), a sage commander who steered Manchester City to their second Premier League title in the 2013-2014 season. His sagacious stewardship navigated the tempestuous waters of competition, leading the club to a symphony of triumph that reverberated across the ages.

In this beautiful dance of managers, linked within the epic narrative of Manchester City's exploits, their names resound through the divine vaults of eternity. A kaleidoscope of beauty, where an enigmatic aura captivates with fervor, a testimony to the legendary club's tenacious soul.

Players

Tommy Johnson

(b.1901 – d.1973)

Johnson was a prolific striker for Manchester City and played a crucial role in the club's success during the 1920s.

The mysterious luminary from Dalton-in-Furness, England, Thomas Clark Fisher Johnson, spreads an aura of intrigue and interest over the enormous world of football. Born on August 19, 1901, his name resonates like an intriguing song, enchanting the hearts and thoughts of fans all over the world. A legendary career stretching from 1919 to 1939, wrapped in an ethereal dance that defied age, enriched with hidden twists at every turn. Johnson's incredible footballing voyage exceeded earthly limits on January 28, 1973, at the ancient age of 71, leaving a path of light that blazed like stars as he departed this world in the vibrant city of Manchester, England. His sheer presence on the pitch, at 5 feet 9 inches tall, was a mesmerizing spectacle, comparable to a dazzling star illuminating the infinite sky.

In the mystical crucible of youth, Johnson's enthralling journey commenced, honing his prodigious skills at Dalton Athletic and Dalton Casuals, where the seeds of greatness were sown, awaiting extraordinary transformation. Ascending to the realm of seniority in 1919, he embarked on a remarkable voyage, traversing the vastness of football's domains until the epochal year of 1939.

Witness the fascinating enclaves of his illustrious career, wherein he graced the hallowed turf for various revered teams, sparking an inferno of passion and devotion among ardent fans. Manchester City beckoned him from 1919 to 1930, a memorable liaison that bore witness to an astonishing 328 appearances and a mesmerising tally of 158 goals, a symphony of brilliance forever etched into the annals of eternity.

An tremendous metamorphosis awaited him, and his astonishing journey began with Everton, lasting from 1930 until 1934. He decorated the pitch with 146 appearances and illuminated the game with 56 goals within the sacred sanctum of this illustrious club, an astonishing alignment that left fans and opponents alike in awe of his exceptional prowess.

As the stars of destiny realigned, Johnson's radiant brilliance graced Liverpool from 1934 to 1936. Within the revered realms of this iconic club, he contributed 36 appearances and crafted 8 goals, a fascinating epoch that added yet another captivating chapter to his already storied career.

In the embrace of time, Johnson's awe-inspiring journey reached its conclusion with Darwen, where his brilliance continued to shine unabated. Throughout this exceptional odyssey, he participated in an astounding 511 matches and notched an otherworldly 222 goals, a numerical puzzle that defies the very laws of comprehension.

Amidst the mystical aura, Johnson adorned the sacred attire of the revered England national team, an extraordinary honor bestowed upon him from 1926 to 1933. Within the field of international competition, he earned 5 caps and astonishingly scored 5 goals, an enigmatic statistic that echoes through the corridors of eternity.

In the grand tapestry of football's intricate history, Thomas Clark Fisher Johnson stands as an enigma wrapped in an enigma, a captivating presence that transcends the confines of mere time and space. His remarkable legacy, akin to a fascinating phenomenon, streaks across the illustrious annals of footballing lore, forever etched in the beating hearts of fans and inscribed into the chronicles of this beautiful sport.

Billy Meredith
(b.1874 - d.1958)

Step into the fascinating world of William Henry Meredith, a Welsh football virtuoso whose name echoed through the ages. Revered as one of the early luminaries of the sport, he graced the hallowed grounds of Manchester City and Manchester United, leaving an indelible mark on the beautiful game.

Billy Meredith on Left

Meredith's performances were nothing short of spectacular, catapulting him to the status of a superstar. He was a maestro on the pitch, a masterful orchestrator of triumphs. With unrivaled flair and finesse, he conquered

English football, clinching every domestic trophy that came his way. His astonishing record boasted an impressive 48 caps for Wales, where his lightning-fast strikes found the back of the net 11 times, propelling his nation to glory on two occasions in the revered British Home Championship.

Positioned strategically as an outside right, Meredith's arsenal of skills was awe-inspiring. Dribbling with an almost mystical grace, his passes were akin to poetry in motion. His crosses carried the precision of a sharpshooter, while his shots reverberated with power and precision. But it wasn't just his prodigious talent that set him apart—it was his trademark habit of chewing on a toothpick during games, an eccentricity that etched his image into the collective memory of fans worldwide.

Across an astonishing span of 27 seasons in the Football League, from 1892 to 1924 (excluding the tumultuous years lost to the ravages of the First World War and banishment in the 1905–06 season for attempting to influence an opposing player), Meredith's impact reverberated with 194 goals in 740 league and cup appearances. His journey commenced at Chirk before he arrived at Northwich Victoria in 1892. However, it was his momentous transfer to Manchester City in 1894 that truly ignited his career, as he boldly embraced the path of professionalism in January 1895. Leading the team with unwavering dedication, Meredith proudly guided Manchester City to their inaugural major triumph, securing a 1–0 victory over Bolton Wanderers in the illustrious 1904 FA Cup Final.

Yet destiny would lead Meredith down a different path, beckoning him to join the ranks of Manchester United in May 1906. However, his ascent to greatness was marred by controversy, as a ban for offering a bribe of £10 (£10 was worth approx. £800 or 30 days wages for a skilled tradesman of the time). Aston Villa's formidable half-back, Alex Leake, clouded his legacy. Nevertheless, he rose above the shadows, ascending to the pinnacle of success with Manchester United, securing the league title in both 1907–08 and 1910–11. Adding to his laurels, the FA Cup gleamed in his grasp in 1909, accompanied by two prestigious FA Charity Shields. Moreover, Meredith played a pivotal role in establishing the Players' Union, a trailblazing precursor to the revered Professional Footballers' Association, championing the rights and welfare of players.

In an extraordinary twist of fate, Meredith's story came full circle when he returned to Manchester City in 1921, defying time itself at the remarkable age of 47. With an unwavering spirit, he graced the pitch for another 32 games, his presence a testament to his undying passion for the sport. As he finally hung up his boots in 1924, he etched his name in the annals of football history as the oldest player ever to represent Manchester City, Manchester United, and Wales. Beyond his playing days, he ventured into the realm of hospitality, running the renowned Stretford Road Hotel, while also lending his wisdom as a coach to the short-lived Manchester Central.

The legend of William Henry Meredith lives on, a dazzling beacon that illuminates the legacy of football's early icons. His tale reminds us of the timeless allure of the game, where brilliance and eccentricity intertwine to create indelible memories that transcend generations.

Eric Brook

(b.1907– d.1965)

Brook is the all-time leading goal scorer for Manchester City, having scored a remarkable 178 goals in his career. He was a key figure during the inter-war period.

Eric Brook, born in 1907 in Mexborough, Yorkshire, is a legendary figure in the history of Manchester City! He started his football journey at Barnsley but quickly caught the eye of our beloved club. In 1928, he made his move to Maine Road and helped City secure promotion as Second Division Champions. Remember that 5-3 victory against Clapton Orient? Brook scored his first goal for City in that thrilling match!

Oh, Eric Brook was a force to be reckoned with! Making a staggering 493 appearances for City in league and cup competitions, he scored a remarkable 158 league goals and 19 FA Cup goals. Talk about power! With his robust physique, he was known as "hard as nails." But that's not all—Brook was more than just a winger; he was a versatile roving forward who even stepped in as goalkeeper on a few occasions. What a man!

His skills and prowess earned him 18 England caps and numerous appearances at representative level. And let's not forget his impact in helping City reach successive FA Cup Finals. Despite the disappointing 3-0 defeat against Everton in 1933, he made history by wearing the number 12 shirt for the first time in an FA Cup Final. But our triumph came in 1934 when we beat Portsmouth 2-1, thanks in no small part to Eric Brook!

Now, let's talk about that jaw-dropping goal against Stoke City in the quarter-finals. It was a match witnessed by a record-breaking crowd of 84,569 fans, and Brook unleashed a thunderous long-range effort that defied gravity! The ball seemed to change direction in mid-air, leaving the Stoke net rattled. Many still consider it the greatest Manchester City goal of all time! Goosebumps, anyone?

In the glorious 1936/37 season, Brook played every single game as City clinched their first-ever League Championship title. What a moment! Unfortunately, the following year saw our beloved club relegated to the Second Division. But let's not dwell on that—Eric Brook's legacy lives on!

Before Sergio Agüero surpassed him, Eric Brook's record of 177 goals stood for a remarkable 78 years! In 2004, he was rightfully inducted into the prestigious Manchester City Hall of Fame, cementing his status as a true City legend.

Beyond his City career, Brook's football journey was cut short by the Second World War. In 1940, he suffered a serious injury that left him unable to safely head the ball. Despite the setback, he continued to contribute to society, working as a coach driver, a barman, and a crane operator. Sadly, he passed away in 1965 at the young age of 57.

Eric Brook will forever hold a special place in the hearts of Manchester City fans. His incredible goals, versatility, and unwavering dedication to the club will be cherished for generations to come. Thank you, Eric Brook, for being a true City legend!

Bert Trautmann
(b.1923 – d.2013)

Bert became a legendary figure at Manchester City. He famously played the 1956 FA Cup Final with a broken neck and went on to win the cup, earning immense respect and admiration from fans.

In the vibrant tapestry of Manchester City's football history, a figure of utmost eminence emerges - Bert Trautmann, whose birth on the 22nd of October in 1923 graced the city of Bremen, Germany. A captivating tale weaves through his journey, brimming with brilliance on the football pitch, profound acts of reconciliation, and the transformative essence of forgiveness.

Setting flight as a goalkeeper for local clubs, Trautmann's trajectory encountered disruption during the tumultuous outbreak of World War II. Like an unexpected twist, the call of duty propelled him into the realm of a paratrooper, putting his football aspirations on an unforeseen hiatus. The pivotal year of 1945 witnessed an unprecedented shift as British forces captured him, altering the very course of his existence.

Within the confines of captivity, Trautmann's remarkable goalkeeping prowess radiated like a dazzling gem within an English prisoner-of-war camp, beckoning the attention of scouts and enchanting spectators with a performance that defied the odds. Freed in 1949, he found sanctuary and new purpose at Manchester City, where a footballing legacy spanning 15 memorable years began to etch its indelible mark.

Amidst skepticism surrounding his German roots, his artistry on the field stood as a testament to his worth, silencing critics and propelling him into the league of celebrated players. A formidable presence, brave and agile, he commanded the penalty area with a grace that left adversaries in awe. The crowning moment arrived during the iconic 1956 FA Cup final, where a spectacle of unwavering determination unfolded as he played through a neck injury, leading Manchester City to a triumphant 3-1 victory.

Over the course of his illustrious tenure, spanning more than 500 appearances for the club, Trautmann's unwavering dedication and professionalism transformed him into a wellspring of inspiration, resonating with fans and fellow players alike. The celestial year of 1956 heralded a groundbreaking achievement, as he secured his place in history as the first goalkeeper to be honored with the prestigious Football Writers' Association Footballer of the Year award, an accolade that testified to his exceptional skill and profound impact on the beautiful game.

Even after the final whistle of his playing days, the strings of connection to Manchester City endured, woven into the very fabric of his being. Embracing the roles of ambassador and coach, he ventured into the noble mission of fostering unity and understanding between Germany and England, leaving an indelible legacy that traversed borders.

The enigmatic story of Bert Trautmann's remarkable journey stands as a resonating testament to the transformative power of forgiveness and reconciliation. Unyielding in the face of formidable challenges, he emerged as a symbol of unity, the architect of a legacy that dismantled barriers and etched its brilliance in the annals of footballing lore.

Alan Arthur Oakes
(b.1942)

Oakes holds the record for the most appearances for Manchester City, having played an impressive 680 matches for the club. He was a loyal servant and a dependable midfielder.

Alan Arthur Oakes, a maestro of footballing brilliance, graced the hallowed confines of Manchester City's realm from 1959 to 1976. Born on the 7th of October in 1942, the tapestry of Manchester, England, bestowed upon him the appellation of Alan Oakes, forever enshrined among the pantheon of the club's all-time greats. An enigmatic odyssey unfolded, adorned with records, as he traversed the spectrum of a long and successful career with the team.

Embarking upon his footballing journey within Manchester City's youth system, Oakes ascended to the firmament of the first-team echelon in 1959. His emergence as a talented midfielder, a virtuoso of technical brilliance, vision, and control over the game's tempo, captivated gazes. Through the epochs of the 1960s and 1970s, he emerged as a linchpin, a constellation that illuminated Manchester City's squad, bestowing success upon the club.

The height of his achievements materialized during the 1967-1968 season, where triumph adorned him. Manchester City, guided by his artistry in the midfield, secured the First Division title, a moment that dissolved a drought of over three decades. Oakes' orchestration, a beacon of stability and creativity, earned admiration, as his passing ability and accuracy in long-range shots bedazzled onlookers.

Astonishing longevity marked his tenure at Manchester City, as he graced the arena a staggering 680 times in all competitions, a record that resounds across the ages. Whispers bestowed him the moniker "Mr. Manchester City," an honour befitting his dedication and loyalty, rendering him a favorite among supporters, an icon of magnitude.

Among accolades, Oakes' talent also beckoned him to represent the England national team. Between 1965 and 1966, he earned the honor of four caps, unveiling his talent on the international stage. Competition and injuries, however, tinted his international career with brevity.

The chapter of Manchester City bid farewell to Oakes in 1976, as he embarked upon brief sojourns with various lower-league clubs before the curtain descended upon his professional footballing journey. Yet, the impact and influence he bestowed upon Manchester City's annals remain etched within the tapestry. In the sanctum of the Manchester City Hall of Fame, his name was inscribed, a tribute to his contributions to the club's heritage.

Alan Oakes' legacy, a testament to his virtuosity as a talented midfielder and his record-breaking achievements at Manchester City, firmly entrenches him within the pantheon of the club's greatest players. His technical brilliance, professionalism, and unwavering commitment continue to reverberate through the corridors of the club's history, an inspiration that ignites the aspirations of future generations of players and fans.

Mike Summerbee
(b.1942)

Summerbee was a skillful winger and a key member of Manchester City's successful teams in the late 1960s and early 1970s, contributing with goals and assists.

Mike Summerbee, an enigmatic force of footballing wizardry, etched an enduring legacy within the hallowed realms of Manchester City Football Club! His arrival graced the world on December 15, 1942, inspiring our beloved team with the brilliance of a winger extraordinaire. From the late 1960s to the early 1970s, Summerbee's enchantment upon the pitch electrified City fans, propelling our club to the most glorious of heights.

The revelation of Summerbee's skills was swift upon joining our ranks in 1965. His arsenal, a blistering velocity that defied norms, a mesmerizing dribbling that hypnotized defenders, and pinpoint crosses that defied precision, rendered him a nightmare for the opposition. Assembling with the legendary trio, the "Holy Trinity," his counterparts Colin Bell and Francis Lee, they fused greatness, painting tales of triumph upon Manchester City's tapestry.

Summerbee's odyssey reached a climax during the 1967-1968 season, the start of an era that ended a 30-year drought for the First Division title. His dashes down the wing, faster than shooting stars, and his assists, an alchemy that created historic victories, instilled excitement and pride in City fans.

Left. Mike Summerbee in action. City v Newcastle United

Yet, his conquests did not cease, as he wielded prowess in the battle for the 1969 FA Cup, completing the domestic double. An assist in the final, an exhibition of his incredible talent, forever enshrined his name within City folklore, a legend that shall echo through the ages.

His tenure embraced 445 appearances, a testament to his unwavering commitment, leaving his essence on the blue side of Manchester with each endeavor. A work rate and versatility endeared him to the fans, and his name reverberates through the air, resounding with pride.

Beyond boundaries, he lent his talents to the England national team, earning eight caps that bore the badge of distinction. The cosmos grieved as he narrowly missed a place in the 1970 World Cup squad, yet his impact leading to the tournament still shines.

Since his boots rested in retirement in 1975, Summerbee's presence persisted, embraced within the City family. As a football pundit, he illuminated with insights, while his role as an ambassador embodied the true spirit of Manchester City, perpetuating his love for the game.

The name of Mike Summerbee, an anthem of our golden era, resonates with reverence among passionate City fans. His talent, passion, and dedication continue to inspire, a beacon guiding the aspirations of souls. With gratitude, we thank you, Mike, for your contributions to our beloved club. Forever, you shall be a hero within our hearts!

Tony Book

(b.1934)

Book, a versatile defender, was the captain of Manchester City during their most successful period. He led the team to numerous trophies, including the league title, FA Cup, and League Cup.

1970 League Cup Final Winner

Tony Book, an illustrious icon etched within the captivating lore of Manchester City! His reign spanned the epoch of 1966 to 1974, a celestial dance upon the hallowed pitch, where passion and dedication intermingled in an unrivaled display. Born on the auspicious September 23, 1934, this extraordinary defender embodied virtue, donning the sky-blue jersey with unwavering pride.

As he embraced our cherished club at the age of 31, a treasure trove of experience and wisdom accompanied his arrival. Commencing his City odyssey in the latter chapters of life, he promptly erected a formidable fortress at the heart of our defence. A tapestry of tactical brilliance woven into his defensive prowess, illuminating the path for all to marvel.

Under Book's captaincy, Manchester City soared to greatness, an exhilarating ascent to the coveted First Division title in 1968. The arid drought was vanquished, and our club bathed in the resplendent glory of triumph. A lighthouse of leadership charting the course, uniting souls in a symphony of success.

Yet, more marvels unfold! In 1969, Book orchestrated another momentous conquest - the FA Cup. His towering presence akin to a colossus, unyielding determination sparking the fire that propelled the team to lift the revered trophy. Pride and joy ablaze in our hearts, as Tony Book epitomized the essence of a true captain, unswayed by the tempest of challenges.

Even after death, Book remained loyal to Manchester City. He gave knowledge as manager and ambassador, creating the club's spirit and fostering the constellation of City stars. His unshakable commitment outshines even the galaxy as a model of greatness.

Tony Book's contributions merited laudation, as he claimed the pioneering spot inducted into Manchester City's illustrious Hall of Fame. This honor, a tribute to his profound impact upon the annals of our history, solidifies his legacy.

We, fervent City fans, exalt Tony Book to great heights, for he embodies the spirit that courses through Manchester City's veins. His leadership, passion, and unyielding commitment resound in echoes, immortalizing him as a true legend. His name resonates with resounding pride, echoing from the fervent stands.

In gratitude, we extend our heartfelt thanks to Tony Book for his unwavering service to our beloved club. His contributions shall be eternally celebrated, and his legacy shall fuel the flames of inspiration for generations of City fans. An icon, forever etched in the iridescent fabric of Manchester City's illustrious history.

Colin Bell
(b.1946 – d.2021)

Bell, known as "The King of the Kippax," was an influential midfielder and one of the greatest players in Manchester City's history. He possessed exceptional skills, vision, and goalscoring ability.

Colin Bell, the unstoppable King of the Kippax! As I say the sacred name of this famous force, an emotional tornado engulfs my Manchester City heart. Bell's impact on our beloved club has gone beyond comprehension, carving his name in the hearts of City supporters all across the world.

On the date of February 26, 1946, Bell graced Manchester City with his presence, soaring to heights of popularity among the fans with swiftness. His skills, a symphony of vision and versatility on the pitch, left us awestruck. Breathtaking goals, chances created, and a tempo dictated - Bell's ability knew no bounds.

Colin Bell, the embodiment of the complete midfielder, a force that defies reckoning. His stamina, athleticism, and technical brilliance rendered him a phenomenon. His prowess to glide past opponents, dancers caught in his wake. Iconic goals, celebrations that echo in the annals of time.

In his era at City, Bell's presence propelled us to success. A key to the team that unlocked the First Division title in 1968, a triumph that brought ecstasy to City fans long yearning for glory. His performances reached new heights, instrumental in our cup conquests.

The climax of Bell's tale emerged in the 1970 League Cup final. Against West Bromwich Albion, he unveiled his artistry with a goal, a masterpiece etching his greatness. A moment transcending memories, forever etched in our minds.

Tragically, a twist of fate truncated Bell's career in 1975, an injury that sent shockwaves through our hearts. Yet, undeterred, his spirit remained radiant. Bell, a figure of adoration, basking in the outpouring of support from fans, love a testament to his profound impact on our existence.

City fans, in their passion, hold Colin Bell in reverence. His dedication, humility, and unwavering loyalty have enshrined him as a legend. The Colin Bell Stand at the Etihad Stadium, a shrine, fittingly immortalizes his legacy.

We, the passionate City fans, are eternally grateful for the memories gifted by Colin Bell. He embodies the essence of Manchester City, a symbol of the blue side of Manchester. His name echoes from the stands, his legacy inspiring generations of City players and fans.

Thank you, Colin Bell, for your incomparable contributions to our beloved club. Forever our King, an eternal symbol of Manchester City's greatness.

Francis (Franny) Henry Lee
(b.1944)

Lee was a highly talented forward who played a vital role in Manchester City's success, scoring crucial goals and providing a significant attacking threat.

Oh, behold the enigmatic Francis Lee, an icon shrouded in mysteries and revered by the fervent Man City enthusiasts! His presence in the 1960s and early 1970s etched an indelible mark on the team and its supporters, an ineffable impact defying all attempts at explanation.

Lee, a forward of unparalleled talent, unrivaled in goal-scoring. His impact on the pitch beyond the reach of comprehension. Nightmares plagued opposing defenders when faced with his speed and agility, and in every match, magic seemed to course through the air.

His passion for the club burned like a fire within him. With pride, he donned the City shirt, each step revealing his unyielding dedication to the team. Fans, in their devotion, felt the resonance of his commitment, and the energy of Lee electrified Maine Road, with chants of his name resonating through the stands.

Lee's goal-scoring record stood pivotal to Manchester City's success. In clashes, his goals proved crucial; in high-pressure situations, he struck with precision, seemingly blessed with the gift of finding the net at the perfect moment.

The pinnacle of his career, the I moment when he played a role in guiding Manchester City to the First Division title in the 1967-1968 season. His goals proved instrumental in securing the championship, an achievement etched forever in the c memory of Man City fans, a testament to Lee's talent and unwavering dedication.

Off the field, Lee's charisma and connection with fans knew no bounds. He understood the significance of supporters, making efforts to interact with them. Embracing the club's traditions and values.

He became a true symbol of Manchester City.

Even after retiring from the realm of professional football, Francis Lee remained an eternal advocate, his passion for Manchester City undiminished.

Francis Lee playing a league match against Arsenal

His contributions to the team's success and his unswerving love for the club earned him an reverence among fans. His legacy, a timeless tapestry woven into the history of Manchester City Football Club.

In the eyes of a passionate Man City fan, Francis Lee transcended the boundaries of a mere great player, becoming an embodiment of the spirit, passion, and dedication that define the club. A representation of everything that makes being a Manchester City fan an experience. His contributions to the team continue to be a cause for eternal celebration, cherished in the boundless expanse of perpetuity.

Georgi Kinkladze
(b.1973)

Kinkladze, a skillful midfielder, was a fan favorite for his dribbling ability and creativity. He produced moments of brilliance and is remembered for his technical skills.

Oh, the enigmatic Georgi Kinkladze, a captivating enchanter whose presence left an indelible mark on the fervent hearts of Manchester City fans. His aura remains shrouded in mystery, remembered as a manifestation of unparalleled skill and excitement, gracing the hallowed grounds of the Etihad Stadium with his awe-inspiring prowess.

Back in 1995, Kinkladze's arrival ignited a blaze of anticipation among the fanbase, his flair and creativity on the pitch captivating all who had the privilege to witness it. Like a cosmic whirlwind, he mesmerized with his dribbling skills, leaving onlookers awestruck by the celestial finesse displayed in his every move.

Let us not forget the standout moment of Kinkladze's time at Manchester City! A solo goal against Southampton during the 1995-1996 season showcased the full extent of his talent. From his own half, he weaved past defenders with mesmerizing ease, before calmly slotting the ball into the net, as if guided by some force. It was a display of magic that left fans in awe, marveling at the brilliance of his abilities.

Yet, it was not merely Kinkladze's skills that endeared him to the passionate Man City fans; it was the ineffable love he held for the club that truly touched their hearts. Through highs and astral lows, he poured his heart and soul into each match, his passion for the club's success radiating like a beacon. His unyielding commitment and dedication resonated deeply with the fans, who embraced him as one of their own.

Beyond the confines of the field, Kinkladze's connection with fans remained and engaging. Approachable and warm, he graciously invested time to interact with supporters, bestowing them with autographs and capturing moments in pictures. Engaging in chats, he made fans feel valued and appreciated, solidifying his status as a true fan favorite.

Even after parting ways with Manchester City, Kinkladze's bond with the club and its fans endured steadfastly. He fondly reminisces about his time at City, expressing gratitude for the unwavering support he received. His love for the club transcends his playing days, eternally cherished among the supporters to this day.

In the eyes of a passionate Man City fan, Georgi Kinkladze is not merely a player of extraordinary skill, but a figure with an authentic connection to the fans. His passion for the club, both as a player and a fan, elevates him to the icon status in Manchester City's storied history. Even now, his name evokes a sense of excitement and nostalgia among supporters who were blessed to witness his magic on the field.

Shaun Goater
(b.1970)

Goater, a striker, was a prolific goal scorer and a cult hero among Manchester City supporters. He played a significant role in the club's promotion and subsequent success.

Shaun Goater, an embodiment of boundless passion and love for Manchester City, an enigmatic figure whose contributions transcend the boundaries of both club and international football.

Throughout his club career at Manchester City, spanning from 1998 to 2003, Goater etched a mark on the hearts of fans. He arrived when the club languished in the third tier, yet his prowess acted as a powerful force, propelling them back to the Premier League. Goater's goal-scoring ability proved a vital catalyst for their promotion, fans helplessly drawn to the allure of his performances on the pitch.

The passion for Manchester City emanated like cosmic rays from Goater, his commitment to the club's traditions and values a sight to behold. His work ethic and determination resonated with the fans, who could feel the palpable energy of his love for the badge in every match. And oh, those goal celebrations, the trademark "Bermuda Triangle" gesture, forever etched in the memory of supporters, further endeared him to their hearts.

Beyond the boundaries of his playing days, Goater's love for Manchester City endures like a flame. As an ambassador, he remains cosmically involved with the club, gracing matches with his presence and passionately representing the team. His aura serves as a constant reminder of his devotion to the club and his desire for continued success.

In the wider arena, Goater represented Bermuda, his homeland, on the international stage. With 36 caps and 32 goals, he achieved a feat for Bermuda football, becoming their all-time leading goal scorer and a inspiration for young aspiring players back home.

In conclusion, Shaun Goater stands as an icon of passion and love, his devotion transcending both club and international football. His contributions and dedication have firmly established him as a figure in Manchester City's storied history. Additionally, Goater's representation of Bermuda serves as a source of inspiration, his influence reaching far beyond the football pitch. A beloved figure among Manchester City fans, he remains a symbol of unwavering devotion.

AND MANY MORE

Uwe Rösler
A burst of popularity as a striker, his goals vital for Manchester City during his tenure. Fans regard him with high esteem.

Richard Dunne
An imposing defender, pivotal in fortifying Manchester City's backline. Known for leadership and defensive prowess.

Paul Dickov
An energetic presence, his knack for crucial goals legendary. His playoff final goal etched in Manchester City's promotion history.

Joe Hart
A crucial guardian between the posts, offering stability and making vital saves during the successful era.

Vincent Kompany
The embodiment of leadership, captaining on and off the field, instrumental in title-winning campaigns.

Shaun Wright-Phillips

A dynamic blur on the wings, his speed and skill contributing goals and assists aplenty.

Peter Doherty

A talented forward, instrumental in league and FA Cup victories during the 1930s.

Sergio Agüero

Aka Kun Agüero, a legendary striker, etching his name in Manchester City's history as all-time leading goal scorer and Premier League hat-trick record holder.

Fernandinho

The reliable anchor in midfield, offering stability and leadership.

Kevin De Bruyne

An exceptional playmaker, visionary passing and long-range shooting defining his presence.

Raheem Sterling

A dynamic and skillful winger, consistently contributing with goals and assists.

Paul Power

A versatile defender, pivotal in Manchester City's 1980s success.

Joe Corrigan

Spending 16 seasons with the club, earning UEFA Cup Winners' Cup and League Cup victories, a neck injury leading to his retirement in 1985.

These are but a few beings among the myriad of managers and players who have graced Manchester City FC throughout their history, their contributions resonating through the club.

PART 10

The Silverware

Major Trophies Won by Manchester City

An intriguing tapestry, weaved with a kaleidoscope of outstanding trophies, is revealed through the winding passages of Manchester City's illustrious past. These trophies were collected from the depths of domestic and international arenas. The club's achievements shine like a constellation of stars in the footballing galaxy, as if drawing a portrait of victories throughout time.

Traveling back through the annals of time, we encounter the runners-up of the Full Members Cup in seasons like 1898/99, 1902/03, 1909/10, and so forth, where they danced on the cusp of glory, tasting both the elation of success and the bitter tang of near-victory. A symphony of close calls, echoing through the epochs of 1927/28, 1946/47, 1965/66, and 1985/86, where they brushed against greatness, yet fell shy of donning the crown.

From the shadows of lower divisions, they ascended like a phoenix, seizing the crown as Second Division/Division One/Championships Winners in the resplendent season of 2001/02. Their ascent, a testament to the relentless spirit and the burning desire for glory.

Amidst their ascendance, however, they occasionally stumbled, finding solace in the role of runner-up. The Division Two Runners-up of 1895/96, 1950/51, and 1988/89, a testimony to the fickleness of fate, as they tasted both the thrill of victory and the pang of falling short.

Yet, fate's mercurial dance revealed its enchanting twist as they soared to triumph, emerging victorious from the crucible of play-offs in the fateful season of 1998/99. A narrative of resilience and fortitude, where they weathered the storm to claim their rightful place in the sun.

The ever-hallowed tradition of the FA Cup bestowed upon them the glory of champions, etching their names in the annals of footballing history. The years of 1903/04, 1933/34, 1955/56, 1968/69, 2010/11, 2018/19, and 2022/23, each marked with a blaze of triumph, a testament to their indomitable spirit and tactical prowess.

But the path to greatness is not without its trials and tribulations. On certain occasions, Manchester City was left grappling with the bitter taste of second place in the FA Cup, the years of 1925/26, 1932/33, 1954/55, 1980/81, and 2012/13 reminding them of the fine line between exaltation and heartbreak.

And let us not overlook the prowess of their women's team, conquering the domain of the FA Women's Super League, their triumph in 2016 a resounding testament to the club's commitment to excellence, both in the men's and women's game.

Amidst the ever-changing tides of football's tempestuous sea, Manchester City's name stands adorned with a coronation of triumphs, a tale of tenacity and tactical artistry that continues to captivate and inspire. As time unfurls its enigmatic tapestry, the club's legacy remains a resonant echo through the ages, a symphony of victory and a testament to the indomitable human spirit.
Women's FA Cup Winners:

Amidst the swirling tapestry of Manchester City's fabled history, brace yourself to navigate through a labyrinth of triumphs, a dizzying kaleidoscope of victories that spans epochs and seasons:

The Women's FA Cup Runners-up, a tantalizing brush with glory that adds a splash of mystique to their mesmerizing narrative. Elusive, yet ever intriguing.

Emerging like specters from the annals of time, the League Cup Winners leave their indelible mark upon the ages, dancing to the beats of seasons past:
1969/70, 1975/76

A symphony of triumphs crescendos through the modern era, each season orchestrating a new chapter of greatness:
2013/14, 2015/16, 2017/18, 2018/19, 2019/20, 2020/21

The Continental Cup Champions seize their throne in the vast continental arena, conquering unseen territories like fearless pioneers:
2014, 2016

Yet, in the ever-shifting tides of competition, the mantle of runners-up embraces them, a tantalizing reminder of the fine line between exaltation and heartbreak:
2017/18

Triumphs of bygone days entwine with present glories, their name waltzing through the annals of time like spectral dancers:

1937/38, 1968/69, 1972/73, 2012/13

The FA Community/Charity Shield becomes a stage for dual triumphs, where they bask in the golden glow of victory:
2018/19, 2019/20

In the epic chronicles of footballing legacy, they etch their grandeur and the irresistible allure of near-glory:
1903/04, 1920/21, 1976/77, 2012/13

The women's team emerges as an unstoppable force, their role as runners-up testifying to their burgeoning prowess and tenacity:
2015, 2017/18, 2018/19, 2019/20, 2020/21

Amidst the ceaseless ebb and flow of football's tides, they seize the crown, crowned champions in their unwavering pursuit of greatness:
1936/37, 1967/68, 2011/12, 2013/14, 2017/18

With each passing season, their accomplishments multiply, a resounding testimony to their tactical acumen and unyielding spirit:
2018/19, 2020/21, 2021/22, 2022/23
In the pantheon of European glory, the European Cup Winners' Cup graces their triumphant mantle, an emblem of past conquests that still shine:
1969/70

Yet even amidst their conquests, the bittersweet flavor of runners-up lingers, an ever-present reminder of the tantalizing nature of victory:
2020/21

But the relentless pursuit of greatness bears rich fruit, as they ascend to the ultimate pinnacle, Champions League victory, where dreams come to fruition:

2022/23

Their might extends to the Premier League 2, where they reign supreme in multiple seasons, an emphatic assertion of dominance:

2020/21, 2021/22, 2022/23

Through the annals of time, they have triumphed as Reserve League Champions, their legacy etched in shining silver, a testament to their perpetual brilliance:

1977/78, 1986/87, 1999/2000

The FA Youth Cup becomes a testament to their nurturing of talent, a shining beacon of hope for the future, where dreams are nurtured and talents blossom:

1985/86, 2007/08, 2019/20

And in the realm of the Under-18 Premier League, they rise as indomitable National Champions, guardians of youthful glory, the architects of tomorrow's triumphs:

2020/21, 2021/22, 2022/23

Such is the enigmatic tapestry of Manchester City's legendary legacy, a symphony of triumphs and near-victories, a living testament to their undying spirit and the burning fervor of their game. As time unfurls its capricious cadence, their resounding imprint resonates through the ages, an ever-evolving symphony that captivates and inspires, a vivid tapestry of dreams woven into the very fabric of football's storied history.

PART 11

A closer look at the Greats

Prominent figures from Manchester City FC's history

As an ardent devotee of the illustrious Manchester City, it is highly probable that you've encountered the names of venerable past legends—eminent figures whose profound significance might have, to some extent, eluded your grasp. Nonetheless, fear not, for I am here to illuminate these extraordinary individuals, thereby endowing you with an unparalleled understanding of the opulent tapestry that adorns the annals of our cherished club's storied history.

In the captivating odysseys of these paragons, you shall behold a mesmerizing amalgamation, an intricate fusion of their unwavering contributions seamlessly interwoven with the indelible legacy of Manchester City. With bated breath, we shall embark upon an expedition, unearthing the quintessential roles they inhabited, conjuring an evocative tableau that epitomizes the resplendent bygone era, a bygone era that eternally defines our extraordinary, resolute club.

Managers

Joe Mercer. O.B.E

(1965-1971):

In the enchanting tapestry of football's annals, a beacon of brilliance emerges—a name adorned with the prestigious Order of the British Empire (OBE). Joseph Mercer, lovingly known as Joe Mercer, graces the world on August 9, 1914, in the hallowed grounds of Ellesmere Port, Cheshire, England. Behold his symphony of success, where life and football history entwine in a magical dance of remarkable achievements and indelible contributions to the sport.

Picture this—verdant fields of Ellesmere Port Town, where Mercer first embraces the mantle of a right-back, blazing a trail to football greatness. In the dazzling kaleidoscope of football destiny, he finds his way to Everton in 1932, his star ascending to illuminate the path to triumph. A formidable presence, a reliable defender, guiding Everton to the pinnacle of glory with the coveted First Division title in the storied 1938-1939 season. Ah, but the capricious winds of fate sweep him into the tempestuous grip of World War II, where an unforeseen detour awaits. Duty calls, and the British Army welcomes a valiant knight to the battlefield.

The post-war dawn heralds a new chapter for Mercer, guiding him to the illustrious ranks of Arsenal in 1946. A crucial cog in their magnificent machinery, orchestrating their triumphant march to the zenith, seizing the First Division title in the resplendent days of 1947-1948. The Three Lions beckon, and Mercer graces the international stage with four illustrious caps between 1938 and 1950, wearing the badge of England with honor and distinction.

Joe on the right with the great Malcolm Allison

Time's sands drift, and a momentous decision materializes—retirement as a player in 1954. But this farewell marks the birth of a new era, a managerial odyssey brimming with brilliance. The winds of destiny, like a serendipitous gust, guide him to the fabled Manchester City, where he assumes the roles of both player-manager and manager. Manchester City's destiny, entwined with Mercer's, embarks on an extraordinary trajectory, unfolding a tale of unparalleled achievement.

Under Mercer's wise and watchful guidance, Manchester City transcends the bounds of possibility. The Second Division beckons, and in the resolute 1965-1966 season, victory embraces them, elevating the club to the storied top flight. A fervent ambition ignites—a flame of glory that has lain dormant for 44 years. Mercer leads his charges with fervor and finesse, and the coveted league title graces their hands in the triumphant 1967-1968 season. History is etched in golden letters, a tale of rapture and redemption.

But wait, the saga does not end there. Mercer's Midas touch adorns the FA Cup in 1969, bestowing upon Manchester City a historic domestic double, a symphony of success reverberating through the ages.

His tactical genius weaves a mesmerizing tapestry of attacking football, the stage for the virtuoso talents of Colin Bell, Francis Lee, and Mike Summerbee the "Holy Trinity" of Manchester City. Beyond the beautiful game, Mercer's spirit thrives, nurturing an oasis of camaraderie, a sanctuary of kinship within the club's embrace.

His coronation as the manager of the England national team in 1974 crowns his storied journey. Yet, amid the applause and acclaim, shadows loom. The 1976 European Championships elude their grasp, a bittersweet chapter in the legacy of a footballing maestro. But with grace, he steps aside, leaving a profound impression on all who crossed his path.

The wheels of fate turn, and the year 1976 heralds the well-deserved accolade—an OBE bestowed upon him, a radiant testament to his dedication and service to the beautiful game
Even in the twilight of his years, Mercer's love affair with football endures. As a scout and advisor, his wisdom adorns the next generation, and his imprint lives on, transcending the limits of time.
But, alas, August 9, 1990, marks the day when the mortal realm bids farewell to a footballing titan. Yet, the echo of his triumphs, the resounding cheers of fans, and the enduring legacy of Joe Mercer shall continue to reverberate through the hallowed halls of football history.

To the faithful, the name Joe Mercer is more than a mere memory—it is an anthem of glory, a tale of a league title after a 44-year wait, a testament to the triumph of passion, spirit, and skill.

In the galaxy of footballing stars, Joseph Mercer shines as a celestial luminary, a name immortalized in the constellation of football legends. As long as the heart of the game beats, the legend of Joe Mercer shall never wane, forever celebrated as an icon of the sport—a living testament to the magic and majesty of football, the beautiful game that enthralls hearts and souls alike.

Roberto Mancini

(2009-2013):

The maestro of Manchester City's resurgence, the architect of their Premier League glory in the 2011-2012 season!

Roberto Mancini, born on November 27, 1964, in Jesi, Italy, transcends the boundaries of football excellence—a former professional player, a highly accomplished manager. His life's journey and football history resonate with symphonies of triumph.

Roberto holding the Premier League Trophy

Back in 1981, the spotlight found him as he joined his hometown club, Bologna. A forward of immense talent, Mancini's star ascended, leading him to Sampdoria in 1982. Guided by the esteemed Vujadin Boškov, triumph embraced them—Coppa Italia glory in 1985, Serie A crown in 1991, a grand dance to the European Cup final in 1992.

Italy beckoned, and Mancini answered, donning the national colors in the 1988 and 1992 European Championships, and the 1990 FIFA World Cup—a warrior of the Azzurri.

In 1997, he ventured to Lazio, his brilliance unabated. Serenading Serie A victory in the 1999-2000 season, and hoisting Coppa Italia and UEFA Cup Winners' Cup in 1999.

The curtain fell on his playing days in 2001, a brief stint at Leicester City marking the end.

The pitch gave way to the touchline, the birth of Mancini the manager. Fiorentina felt his touch, ascending from Serie B to Serie A—a crescendo of triumph.

Inter Milan summoned him, a historic tenure ensues. Three consecutive Serie A titles (2005-2006, 2006-2007, 2007-2008), a duet of Coppa Italia titles—he leads them to the zenith.

Manchester City, in 2009, becomes his canvas, a transformative era unfurls. With resources aplenty, Mancini crafts a formidable squad, the path to glory illuminated. The FA Cup is claimed in 2011—a 35-year drought quenched. Then, a resounding crescendo—a Premier League title after 44 years, seized on the final day of the 2011-2012 season, etching history's pages in bold letters.

The accolades continue—a Community Shield (2012), a League Cup (2014). Yet, like the ebb and flow of the beautiful game, he parts ways with the club in 2013, his hunger for further league titles unsated.

Tactical brilliance and a penchant for winning carve his legacy. Beyond Manchester City, he graces Galatasaray in Turkey, Zenit Saint Petersburg in Russia—the legend of "The Prince" echoes among fans and admirers.

In 2018, the Italian national team beckons, a fresh chapter for Mancini—a resurgence orchestrated. The UEFA Nations League trophy, claimed in 2020-2021, testifies to the revival's success.

Roberto Mancini's tale—narrating remarkable achievements, both as player and manager. Sampdoria, Inter Milan, Manchester City—the Italian national team—each chapter adds to the opus of this esteemed football figure—a symphony of greatness, etched in football's timeless embrace.

Pep Guardiola

(2016-present):

In the vast landscape of football's annals, one name shines with resplendent glory—a name that resonates with immense success, a tale of multiple league titles and domestic cups.

Pep Guardiola, born Josep Guardiola Sala on January 18, 1971, emerges as a luminary—a former professional player and a triumphant manager whose life's symphony is adorned with remarkable achievements, tactical brilliance, and an unwavering commitment to the captivating allure of possession-based football.

Guardiola's journey commences at FC Barcelona's hallowed La Masia, the crucible of his footballing prowess. The year 1990 witnesses his first-team debut, and in the blink of an eye, he rises—a gifted midfielder, a maestro of technical finesse, vision, and breathtaking passing acumen. The 1990s dance to Barcelona's rhythm, and Guardiola stands at the heart of their success—six La Liga titles and the UEFA Champions League crown in the illustrious 1991-1992 season.

Under the watchful gaze of the esteemed Johan Cruyff, Guardiola embodies the essence of the "Dream Team." "Tiki-taka" finds its orchestrator, and Barcelona's dominance owes much to Guardiola—the architect of play, the midfield maestro.

His journey meanders to Italy's Serie A, a brief sojourn with Brescia, before returning to Spain's embrace at Al-Ahli—a chapter that marks the finale of his playing days in 2006.

Yet, Guardiola's odyssey is not bound by the pitch, for destiny beckons—a touchline awaits. Coaching beckons, and he answers the call—Barcelona's youth teams witness the blossoming of a future manager. In 2007, the first-team reins are handed to him, a golden chapter ensues.

Guardiola's era as Barcelona's manager unveils an epoch of glory—a footballing renaissance. Possession reigns supreme, intricate passing becomes a hallmark, and relentless pressing defines their essence. Unprecedented success ensues—La Liga titles flow like a torrential downpour

(2008-2009, 2009-2010, 2010-2011), UEFA Champions League crowns grace them (2008-2009, 2010-2011), domestic cups sparkle in their cabinet.

A brief hiatus follows in 2013, but the allure of coaching beckons, and Bayern Munich embraces him. From 2013 to 2016, the Bundesliga echoes with their dominance—three consecutive titles are claimed.

In 2016, a new chapter unfolds—the hallowed grounds of Manchester City embrace him, the Premier League beckons. Under his guidance, a symphony of success echoes through the Etihad—Premier League triumphs abound (2017-2018, 2018-2019, 2020-2021), FA Cups, and League Cups are secured—the colors of triumph painted on their canvas.

Guardiola's canvas is a spectacle—a fluidity that mesmerizes, positional play that mystifies, and a relentless pursuit of dominance. His tactical acumen crafts masterpieces, unlocking the brilliance of his players—his impact, a symphony of influence, an era-defining legacy.

Not only a club magician, but Guardiola also graced the Spanish national team, leading them to glory in the 2009 UEFA European Under-21 Championship.

Pep Guardiola's life's tapestry dances to a distinctive rhythm—an indelible impact on the beautiful game as a player and manager, etched in the hallowed halls of football's chronicles, forever celebrated as a luminary—a timeless tale of excellence and footballing artistry.

Malcolm Allison

(1972-1980):

Malcolm Alexander Allison's journey through the intricate web of English football is a tale of dual roles—player and manager, an architect of the team's triumphs, and a maven of innovation.

Born on September 5, 1927, in Dartford, Kent, England, Allison's legacy reverberates through the annals of the sport. However, the final curtain descended on October 14, 2010, marking the end of a colorful life, extinguished by the clutches of lung cancer at the age of 83.

As a player, Allison's flight began as a wing-half for Charlton Athletic in 1946. Yet, destiny beckoned, and his journey wove through the threads of clubs like West Ham United, Leyton Orient, and Brighton & Hove Albion. But alas, fate dealt a cruel hand—a knee injury truncated his playing dreams, propelling him into the corridors of coaching and management.

The tapestry of his managerial career is embroidered with the gilded colors of Manchester City—a pinnacle of success carved alongside Joe Mercer. Together, they orchestrate the symphony of victory—conquering the Football League First Division title in 1967-68, seizing the FA Cup in 1969, and claiming the League Cup in 1970.

But it is Allison's managerial panache that sets him apart—a flamboyant streak etched in fashion, sporting fedora hats and sheepskin coats on the touchlines. Yet, beyond sartorial elegance lies innovation—an audacious pioneer in statistical analysis and sports science in English football. The realm of computers weaves into his strategy—a mastery of player performance and fitness levels, like a visionary ahead of his time.

A chapter closes at Manchester City, draped in disagreement with the board, leading him to helm other clubs. Crystal Palace witnesses his magic, and Sporting Lisbon embraces his managerial touch.

But the canvas of his life is vibrant, a kaleidoscope of extravagance—a penchant for the finer things in life, fine dining, casinos, and the allure of high living. The prism of media attention dances upon his personal life, occasionally veiling his managerial exploits.

Yet, the curtain falls on October 14, 2010, lung cancer's grip unwavering—a battle fought valiantly, but fate casts its verdict. At the age of 83, the final whistle blows—a legend of English football takes his bow.

Amidst the controversies that dappled his life, Allison's indelible mark on English football shines bright—an architect of innovative coaching methods. A symphony of tactical brilliance conducts the field—attacking football, possession-based and captivating.

A maverick in data analysis, statistical sorcery reigns supreme. He dissects opponents, exploiting weaknesses, devising match strategies—data-driven precision, a pioneering vision.

The marriage of sports science and football, like alchemy in his hands, players' physical prowess refined to perfection. He crafts peak condition with technological finesse—stamina, speed, and strength measured with scientific precision.

The tapestry of his success thrives on detail—meticulous preparation, opposition study, a blueprint of vulnerabilities, and strengths nullified. The artist of strategy, a maestro of planning.

His aura inspires loyalty—a charismatic figure, authoritative and connected with his players. Man-management, an art wielded with mastery, a united squad under his tutelage.

The human psyche, a realm he conquers—psychological motivation, belief instilled, a desire to conquer the world, a winning mentality etched in his teams.
A legacy of innovation and forward-thinking, his mark on Manchester City an enduring testament. A maven of coaching, a luminary in the world of football—a beacon of inspiration for future generations of managers.

The chronicles of Malcolm Allison—a player, a manager, an innovator, forever etched in football's tapestry, an icon of the sport—a lasting impact on the beautiful game, a symphony of excellence and tactical artistry.

Manuel Pellegrini (2013-2016):

In the labyrinth of football's history, a name emerges—a maestro of managerial brilliance. Manuel Pellegrini, born on September 16, 1953, in Santiago, Chile, a revered figure in the world of football.

His journey begins on the verdant fields of Chile, a center-back in his playing days, before seizing the reins of coaching. The trajectory of his managerial odyssey traces through Chilean football, exploring uncharted territory in Argentina, Ecuador, and Spain.

But it is in Villarreal where recognition blooms, a foray into the UEFA Champions League semifinals in the 2005-2006 season—a testament to his tactical prowess and vision.

A dance with destiny leads him to the grand stage—Real Madrid, an orchestra of talent at his disposal. A record-breaking 96 points adorn La Liga in the 2009-2010 season, a symphony of dominance, though the title narrowly eludes their grasp, clutched by the hands of Barcelona.

But the zenith of his managerial legacy adorns the cerulean blue of Manchester City—a transformative reign from 2013 to 2016. The Premier League beckons, a historic title etched in golden letters—the 2013-2014 season, a climax of drama, the championship secured on the season's final breath.

The canvas of Manchester City's football sways to his brushstroke—a palette of attacking prowess, goals soaring through the heavens—a record number in Premier League history.

Calm and composed, Pellegrini's demeanor exudes wisdom—tactical acumen woven into every move, disciplined defense, an attacking flair that captivates.

Manuel Pellegrini Directing his team to another win

Yet, beyond the tactical symphony, it is his touch of alchemy—man-management prowess that leaves an indelible impression. A positive aura envelops the squad—a cohesive unit bonded by the alchemy of their maestro.

As time flows and events unfold, my data is limited, and the present remains a mystery. Manuel Pellegrini's journey, a tapestry of triumphs and accomplishments, a master of his craft, a revered figure in football's pantheon of managerial greats.

PART 12

ROUTE TO THE 22/23 CHAMPIONS LEAGUE FINAL

Can we dream?

2022-23 Season: What a remarkable triumph for Manchester City as they clinched the Premier League title for an astonishing third consecutive time, leaving second-place Arsenal trailing by a margin of five points.

And that's not all; the blues triumphed over their fierce rivals, Manchester United, with a 2-1 victory in the thrilling FA Cup final, securing the crown of England's domestic club competition.

Guiding this exceptional journey was none other than the mastermind, Pep Guardiola. With his tactical brilliance, Guardiola has now steered Manchester City to a staggering five Premier League titles.

Let's not forget his past achievements, as he previously conquered the UEFA Champions League twice during his tenure with FC Barcelona in 2009 and 2011.

When it comes to netting goals, Erling Haaland emerged as the undisputed hero. Making his mark in his debut season at Manchester City, Haaland lit up the pitch with an incredible tally of 52 goals across all competitions during the unforgettable 2022-23 campaign.

Notably, he etched his name in Premier League history by smashing the record with an astonishing 36 goals this season alone. Haaland's excellence extended beyond the domestic stage, with 12 goals in 10 appearances in the UEFA Champions League.

Of course, Haaland wasn't the sole driving force behind Manchester City's triumphs. The squad boasted a stellar cast of players, including the phenomenal goalkeeper Ederson representing Brazil, the electrifying forward Jack Grealish donning England's colors, the midfield maestro Kevin De Bruyne, a national gem for Belgium, the versatile Ilkay Gündogan from Germany, the creative Bernardo Silva hailing from Portugal, the composed midfielder Rodri from Spain, and the tenacious defender Nathan Aké representing the Netherlands.

Now, let's rewind and explore Manchester City's path to the grand finale. After emerging victorious from their group stage, they faced a formidable challenge in the form of two German powerhouses: RB Leipzig and Bayern Munich.
Undeterred, Manchester City showcased their might by toppling these giants in the Round of 16 and quarterfinals, respectively.
The crowning moment arrived when they resoundingly defeated the defending UEFA Champions League champions, Real Madrid, with an aggregate score of 5-1 in the semifinals.

Switching gears, let's delve into the realm of Inter Milan. In the 2022-23 season, Inter Milan secured a respectable third place in Serie A, finishing 18 points behind the champions Napoli and a mere two points adrift of second-placed Lazio.
Their silver lining came in the form of the Coppa Italia, Italy's prestigious domestic club competition. The team emerged victorious in the final, edging out Fiorentina with a hard-fought 2-1 triumph.

At the helm of Inter Milan's recent successes stands Simone Inzaghi. In just two seasons, Inzaghi has masterminded back-to-back victories in the Italian Cup, solidifying his position as a tactical genius.

PART 13

THE FINAL- Are We Allowed Too Dream?

Champions League Final 2023

Manchester City v Inter-Milan

KICK OFF 20.00 10TH June 2023

Its **10pm** in Istanbul and **8pm** in England and on a hot sticky night. The Champions League final kicks off.

Lautaro Martinez getting the ball rolling for Inter.

Game on!!!

0 min We're off on this monumental journey, where history awaits. Manchester City, our beloved club, could become only the second Premier League team to conquer the elusive treble. Let's follow in the footsteps of our city rivals and etch our name in glory, just like Manchester United did in 1999..

2 mins

City's dominance is evident from the start as John Stones launches a quick throw-in. Though Inter swiftly regain possession and push forward, Edin Dzeko falters near the corner flag, unable to keep the ball in play. A goal kick for City fuels our passion for victory!

3 mins

The excitement builds as Erling Haaland bursts forward, perfectly timed with a majestic through ball from our maestro Kevin De Bruyne! With sheer power, he unleashes a shot, soaring high over the bar from a challenging angle. Alas, offside denies us, but the fire in our hearts remains unquenchable!

7 mins

Get ready to witness greatness! Bernardo Silva takes control on the right flank, charging into the penalty area as Federico Dimarco retreats. With skillful finesse, Silva shifts the ball onto his left foot, aiming to curl it into the far corner. Oh, so close! His attempt narrowly misses, igniting our excitement for that elusive goal!

10 mins

Hold your breath, fellow City fans! Hakan Calhanoglu charges towards our penalty area, but our defense stands strong. He passes wide to Federico Dimarco, and Inter swarm the box in anticipation of a cross. But fear not, for our mighty Ruben Dias rises above them all, unleashing a thunderous header to clear the danger! Victory is within our grasp!

12 mins

Heart-stopping moments, but fear not! Ederson's rare stumble gifts Inter a throw-in near our territory. Denzel Dumfries launches it long, causing Ederson to momentarily lose track. Oh, the tension! Martinez keeps it alive, but our hero John Stones swiftly clears the loose ball. Ederson's unconvincing display, yet City remains unscathed. The battle rages on!

15 mins

Oh, the intensity rises as Inter resort to the long ball! They go Route One, launching it high towards Martinez. But fear not, for our defensive titan Ruben Dias steps up and clears the danger with authority! City's resilience shines through, thwarting Inter's desperate attempts. We hold strong in the face of adversity!

16 mins

Oh, what a thrilling start! City has already created the best and only chance of the game. But let's not underestimate Inter! The game's evidence proves they won't be easily overwhelmed by our Premier League dominance. It's still early in this final, and Inter is showing their mettle, matching us stride for stride. Brace yourselves for an epic battle!

18 mins

Ake's long ball, Haaland's header, and Grealish's pursuit! Bastoni rushes to shut him down, denying him the turn, and we win a throw-in. Alas, despite our efforts, it leads to nothing. But fear not, for our spirit remains unyielding! Onward, City, to triumph!

19 min

Oh, the audacity of Brozovic! From a distance, he dares to test our resolve, only to send the ball sailing high over the bar. Martinez, his frustration is plain to see, yearning for that pass instead. But no matter, we stand strong! City's determination will prevail!

22 min

Oh, the drama unfolds! Dimarco falls injured after colliding with our very own Bernardo Silva, but play carries on around him. City charges forward, attempting to break through Inter's defence, but to no avail. Dimarco eventually rises to his feet, frustrated that the referee didn't intervene. Fear not, for he'll live on, and so will our indomitable spirit! Onward, City, to glorious victory!

25 min

Oh, the battle rages on! Barella's foul on our dazzling Grealish sparks fireworks halfway inside Inter's territory. Niggly challenges fly from both sides, hindering the game's fluidity. But fear not, City's resilience shall prevail! Let the passion ignite, for victory is within our grasp!

26 min

Oh, the tension! Ederson's rare misplacement gifts Brozovic a golden opportunity. With lightning speed, he tries to chip the ball over our keeper and into the open goal. But oh, the relief! His effort veers wide, leaving us breathless. Ederson, though uncharacteristically shaky tonight, shall redeem himself. We trust in our heroes! Onward, City, to victory!

27 min

Oh, the anticipation! A glorious chance unfolds! Rodri and De Bruyne weave their magic, exchanging passes with precision. Haaland, the mighty, is unleashed behind the defence. Shooting from a challenging angle, he unleashes his power, but Onana denies him with a sensational leg save. The battle intensifies! City, relentless in pursuit of victory!

30 min

The tension mounts! Our beloved De Bruyne is in need of treatment, battling through what appears to be a hamstring injury. Yet, he carries on, fighting for the cause. Memories of the past haunt us, as he was forced off in the Champions League final two years ago. Tonight, we hope and pray history won't repeat itself.

We stand with you, Kevin! Onward, City, to triumph and redemption!

31 min

Oh, the anticipation builds! Foden, our young star, sheds his substitute's bib, preparing himself just beside our dugout. A sign that spells concern for De Bruyne, who valiantly soldiers on for now. Our hearts ache for our fearless leader, but fear not! City stands united, ready to rally and seize the moment. Onward to glory, with Foden and the entire team by our side!

34 min

Oh, the intensity soars! Gundogan launches a thrilling ball towards the touchline, intended for De Bruyne to chase. He reaches it with his unwavering determination, but alas, his cross goes astray. In that moment, he signals to the bench, signaling that the battle is over for him. And now, a moment of change! Manchester City substitution: Phil Foden enters the stage, replacing the valiant De Bruyne. Let the torch be passed, as our spirits soar with unwavering faith in our heroes! Onward, City, to resounding victory!

37 min

Inter relentlessly press our City warriors, pushing them to their limits with unwavering determination. This tactic proves fruitful, but will they sustain it under the scorching heat? Even at this late hour, Istanbul records 21% Celsius with 60% humidity. Is that a lot? Who's to say, but it feels like an overwhelming challenge. Nevertheless, our spirit remains unyielding! Let the battle rage on, for victory awaits in the face of adversity!

40 min

Oh, the passion ignites! Calhanoglu, fueled by aggression, seizes the ball from Bernardo Silva, deep within Inter's territory. With lightning speed, he charges into our half, igniting the atmosphere. But fear not, for our City warriors converge, creating an impenetrable wall. Calhanoglu succumbs to the traffic, losing possession. Victory is ours to claim! Onward, City, with unyielding spirit!

43 min

Oh, the anticipation rises! City earns a precious free-kick, awarded for Dumfries' foul on our majestic Grealish. In the heat of the moment, Grealish pleads to the ref, urging a booking for his marker. Ah, Jack, your passion is unmatched! Foden steps up, launching the free-kick deep into the fray. Rodri, determined as ever, attempts a cross, only to be thwarted by Martinez's block. The ball ricochets off Rodri, sailing out for a goal kick. The battle continues, each moment pulsating with exhilaration! Come on, City, let's seize our destiny!

45+1 min

Oh, the audacity! Akanji unleashes a left-footed strike from a thunderous distance of 25 yards. The ball soars through the air, fueling our hopes, but alas, it sails over the Inter cross-bar. The near-miss ignites our passion, as victory beckons with each exhilarating moment. Onward, City, with unyielding determination! Let the roar of triumph echo through the stadium!

Half-time: City 0-0 Inter. The battle continues!

Oh, the tension builds as the referee, Szymon Marciniak, signals the end of the first half with resounding blasts of his whistle. The players retreat to the sidelines, catching their breath. Chances have been scarce, but our beloved City had the two best opportunities, courtesy of the magnificent Bernardo Silva and the unstoppable Erling Haaland. Inter sought to exploit an Ederson mistake, but Brozovic's audacious long-range attempt missed its mark. Alas, we suffered a blow as De Bruyne departed due to injury, yet our indomitable spirit persists! Phil Foden steps in, ready to create magic in the second half. Onward, City, to glorious triumph!

Second half begins: City 0-0 Inter. Let's go!

46 min Game on! Manchester City take control of the ball as play resumes. Both teams remain unchanged in personnel.

Let the battle intensify, as our hearts surge with anticipation! Come on, City, show them our relentless spirit!

46 min

The defence stands tall! Dzeko releases a swift, low pass down the right touchline, aiming for the speedy Barella. Yet, our fearless Akanji surges forward, beating the Italian to the ball with unwavering determination. With a confident touch, Akanji swiftly passes it back to the mighty Ederson. City's resilience shines bright as we thwart their advances! Onward, City, with unyielding strength!

47 min

Oh, the drama unfolds! Dimarco falls, clutching his face and the small of his back after Silva disrupts his run. The cunning Italian tries to gain an advantage by backing into Silva as he controls a dropping ball. Yet, fear not, for it was a futile challenge! Dimarco swiftly rises to his feet, ready to resume the battle. The spirit of City prevails, undeterred by their futile attempts. Onward, City, with unyielding tenacity!

49 min

Oh, the opportunity arises! Onana, in the Inter goal, makes a rare mistake, granting Silva a chance to charge into their penalty area from the right. With lightning speed, Silva attempts a pull-back, aiming to unlock their defense. But Acerbi, ever watchful, blocks the maneuver with determination. The stage is set, City! Let our relentless spirit guide us to glory!

50 min

The battle intensifies! Our warrior, Gundogan, is fouled by Calhanoglu, leaving him in need of treatment. But fear not, for our indomitable hero persists, determined to carry on! The referee awards a precious free-kick to City on the halfway line. The stage is set, the moment is ours! Let our might and skill shine through, City! Onward to victory!

53 min The intensity rises! Gundogan charges forward, colliding with Martinez, but play carries on, undeterred.

Moments later, a delightful turn of events! Darmian is rightfully penalized for his foul on the magnificent Grealish, out on the left flank. Ah, the stage is set for Foden's brilliance! But alas, his delivery falls short, lacking its usual precision. Akanji valiantly tries to salvage the situation but fails to keep the ball in play. The ebb and flow of the game, ever thrilling! Onward, City, with unwavering spirit!

54 min

The injustice unfolds! Foden is wrongly penalized just outside the Inter penalty area. Calhanoglu shamelessly throws himself to the ground, while our innocent City substitute happens to be standing nearby. "I didn't touch him!" cries out Foden in exasperation, his frustration echoing the truth. The referee's decision bewilders us all, but fear not, City! Our spirit remains unyielding, our determination unwavering! Rise above, City, for justice shall prevail!.

56 min

It's a game-changer, folks! Inter makes a swap: Lukaku takes the stage, replacing Dzeko, who's given his all with those tireless long legs. In this electric opening hour, Dzeko's left it all on the field. But now, Lukaku emerges, ready to ignite the fire! Brace yourselves, City fans, for the excitement is far from over! Let's cheer our team to victory!

57 min

Lukaku announces his presence with authority, soaring high to win his first header! The ball sails wide, finding Dumfries on the right touchline. But fear not, for our defender Akanji swiftly takes charge, handling the cross with finesse, ensuring no danger befalls us. City's resilience shines through! Onwards, brave warriors! Victory awaits!

59 min

A heart-stopping moment! Ederson and Akanji momentarily tangled up in their communication, leaving Martinez to pounce on a loose ball down the left of our penalty area. Ederson stands tall, blocking the shot from that tight angle! Our goalkeeper's reflexes save the day, ensuring our fortress remains impenetrable. City's resilience shines through! Onwards to triumph, my fellow fans!

60 min

What a dazzling run by Foden! Our talented lad is brought down just a few yards from the Inter penalty area by Barello, earning the first booking of the match. The referee's whistle resounds, but fear not, City fans, as the resulting free-kick doesn't yield immediate results. Nonetheless, we're in high spirits, knowing our boys are hungry for more! Onwards to glory, City!

61 min

Ederson, you had our hearts in our throats! Your little slip-up allowed Martinez a chance at goal, albeit from a tight angle. Pep Guardiola couldn't believe it, dropping to his knees on the touchline in excitement and anxiety. Martinez had options, tempted to pass to Lukaku or Barella, but fear not! Our defence was on point, providing solid cover in the penalty area. City's resilience shines through! We're in for a thrilling ride, my fellow fans! Hold on tight and trust in our team's determination!

64 min

Ruben Dias, what a defensive masterclass! He rises above the rest, unleashing a powerful header to thwart Dimarco's attempt to connect with Lukaku's looping header near our six-yard box. The crowd erupts with cheers as our defensive rock keeps us safe. Our resilience knows no bounds! City's defense stands tall! Let's keep pushing forward, my fellow fans, victory awaits!

67 min

What a brilliant burst of energy from Haaland! He charges towards the Inter penalty area, seeking to unleash a perfect pass into the waiting pocket of space for our maestro Phil Foden. But hold on, Bastoni steps in with a crucial interception, denying our attacking brilliance. Hats off to the Inter defender for his excellent defensive display. The tension rises, but we won't stop fighting! Come on, City!.

GOAL! Manchester City 1-0 Inter (Rodri 68)

What team play by Manchester City! Manuel Akanji starts it off with a brilliant pass to Bernardo Silva, positioned on the byline to the right of the Inter goal.

Silva's pull-back is absolutely inch-perfect, and with pure precision, Rodri hammers the ball past Bastani and Onana, sending it zooming into the back of the net!

The City side of stadium erupts with joy as we take the well-deserved lead! That's how we do it, City! Keep it up!

GOALLLLLLL !!!!!!!!!!!!!!!

An aerial view of Rodri scoring for Manchester City

71 min

Oh my, that was a heart-stopping moment! Inter come inches away from equalizing. Dimarco leaps up and delivers a powerful looping header that smacks against the crossbar from the edge of the six-yard box. The ball ricochets off the woodwork, but guess what? It falls perfectly for Dimarco again, and he unleashes another header towards the goal. But wait! Out of nowhere, an unaware Romelu Lukaku unintentionally blocks the shot with his back! Talk about luck on our side! We can breathe a sigh of relief as our lead remains intact. Come on, City, let's keep pushing!

73 min

Lukaku's shot is nothing but a harmless scuffed effort, straight into the waiting arms of our incredible Ederson! Easy peasy, no trouble at all! Our goalkeeper is rock solid, ready for anything that comes his way. City's defense stands strong, denying any chances for Inter. We're in control, folks! Let's keep the momentum going!

75 min

Oh, what a free-kick by Manchester City! With perfect precision, we curl it into the heart of the Inter penalty area. But wait, their defense manages to head it away, denying us the immediate breakthrough. No worries though, because now it's time for some Inter substitutions! Bellanova and Gozens enter the field, ready to make their mark. It's all happening, folks! The excitement is building, and City is determined to keep the pressure on!

77 min:

Phil Foden, what a magician on the ball! With lightning-fast footwork, he leaves the defender in the dust and bursts into the Inter penalty area. The crowd holds its breath as he sets his sights on the bottom right-hand corner. The shot is unleashed, but Onana, the Inter keeper, reacts with lightning reflexes to make a crucial save. Oh, the drama and excitement! Foden is a force to be reckoned with, and City is knocking on the door, hungry for that goal!

80 min

Pep Guardiola knows how to keep us on the edge of our seats! Poor Kyle Walker, itching to get on the pitch, has been teased for what feels like an eternity. But the moment has arrived! He's ready to unleash his power! And what's this? A City free-kick, wide on the right, thanks to Brozovic's slip-up. The tension builds as Gundogan whips in a tantalizing delivery. But alas, Onana, the Inter keeper, snatches it confidently from the air. The excitement is palpable as we eagerly await Walker's impact on the game! Come on, City!

81 min

What a sight! Our brave John Stones got caught up in a fierce battle with Robin Gosens, and his shirt paid the price with a mighty rip down the side. But fear not, City fans, for our hero Kyle Walker is here to save the day! The substitution is made, and Walker steps onto the field, ready to unleash his speed and strength. Stones may be departing, but let's not forget the incredible performance he put on. What a game it's been! City's determination knows no bounds! Onward to victory!

82 min

What a moment! Romelu Lukaku receives a yellow card for his tackle from behind on our unstoppable force, Ilkay Gundogan. The referee's decision ignites the crowd with excitement as we cheer on our player, rising above the challenge. City's spirit remains unbreakable, and we're ready to conquer the game with passion and determination. Let's go, City!

84 min

Unleashing their firepower, Inter makes a double substitution! Henrikh Mkhitaryan and Danilo D'Ambrosio enter the field, replacing Calhanoglu and Darmian. The anticipation is electrifying as we witness the tactical moves unfolding. It's time for City to rise to the challenge and show our relentless spirit. We're ready to dominate and secure our victory! Come on, City!.

87 min

Nathan Ake, the defensive maestro, reads Mkhitaryan's intentions perfectly and intercepts his attempted pass down the right touchline. The crowd erupts with excitement as Ake showcases his defensive prowess. Our City players are on fire tonight, leaving no room for the opposition to break through. Keep it up, lads! We're dominating this match!

88 min

Oh my word! Ederson, the shot-stopping magician, pulls off an UNBELIEVABLE save! Lukaku's thunderous header from close range seemed destined for the back of the net, but Ederson defies all odds, shuffling across his goal line and making an incredible knee save. It's pure reflexes and agility on display!

But wait, the drama doesn't end there. Brozovic's cross finds Gosens, who nods it across the goalmouth, only for Ederson to parry it away. Ruben Dias, showing nerves of steel, ensures there's no own goal, expertly directing the ball out for a corner with his well-timed header. What a remarkable display of teamwork and composure!

That save from Ederson was simply out of this world. He's proving once again why he's one of the best keepers in the world. And let's not forget, it's also a dreadful miss from the Inter side. They'll be kicking themselves for not capitalizing on that golden opportunity. We're riding high on this thrilling rollercoaster of a match! City's defence is standing strong, and our goalkeeper is an absolute superhero!

90+2 min

We're in the final moments, and it's getting intense! Five minutes of added time, and things are heating up. Haaland and Onana receive yellow cards for their antics on the pitch. Oh, the suspense!

But let's talk about Lukaku. He's still reeling from that missed opportunity with a bullet header from a mere four yards out. Unbelievable! Determined to make amends, he takes a shot from an audacious distance, way out wide. The man's got confidence, that's for sure!

The energy is electric, and every second counts. Will City hold on to their lead? Can Inter turn the tables? The drama continues to unfold, and we're on the edge of our seats, cheering our boys on! This is what football is all about!

90+4 min

Ederson is showing his passion and determination out there! He's booked for a bit of time-wasting, but that won't dampen his spirits. Moments later, he charges off his line like a lightning bolt, soaring high into the air. With unwavering confidence, he snatches the Onana free-kick from deep that was dangerously dropping into our penalty area. What a display of goalkeeping brilliance!

Ederson's reflexes and command of the box are simply outstanding. He's like a superhero guarding our net, leaving no room for doubt or hesitation. His heroics give us that extra boost of excitement and confidence.

The atmosphere is electric as the clock winds down. With Ederson in top form, we feel invincible. This is the epitome of world-class goalkeeping, and we're privileged to have him between our posts. Let's keep pushing forward and secure this victory!

90+5 min Bellanova, with lightning pace, whips in a cross that's met with sheer determination!
The ball ricochets off an opponent's leg and soars high into the air, narrowly missing the target. It's a deflection, resulting in an Inter corner! The tension is mounting as both teams battle it out for supremacy.

We're witnessing a thrilling contest, full of heart-stopping moments and relentless action. Every corner is a chance to seize the advantage, and we're ready to defend our goal with all our might. The crowd roars in anticipation as we hold our breath, eager to see what unfolds next.

Our defence is solid, but Inter is hungry for an equalizer. We must remain focused, anticipate their moves, and respond with swift precision. It's moments like these that define champions, and we won't back down. Let's hold our ground and continue to showcase the strength of our team!

90+6 min

Dimarco delivers an enticing corner towards the near post, and who else but Robin Gosens rises above the rest to get a crucial flick on the ball! It's a heart-stopping moment as the crowd holds their breath in anticipation.
But our extraordinary goalkeeper, Ederson, reacts with lightning-fast reflexes and pulls off an absolutely sensational save! He dives, he stretches, he defies the laws of physics to deny Inter's attempt. It's pure brilliance between the posts!

Rodri, Grealish, Haaland celebrating the goal that made City Treble Winners

The stadium erupts with cheers and applause as Ederson showcases his shot-stopping prowess. He's like a superhero guarding our goal, making the impossible seem effortless. With his incredible skills, he's become the backbone of our defense, instilling fear in the hearts of opposing attackers.

This is the resilience of Manchester City, the never-say-die spirit that fuels our pursuit of victory. We stand strong, unyielding in the face of adversity, knowing that with Ederson guarding our goal, we have an unrivaled advantage.

The crowd roars with excitement, the energy electrifying the atmosphere. Moments like these define our team, reminding the world why we're the unstoppable force in football !

Onwards we march, with Ederson as our last line of defence, ready to conquer any challenge that comes our way

The Treble Complete.

Manchester City are champions of Europe!

WHATS JUST HAPPENED?

Our long-awaited quest for glory is complete, and we've etched our name in football history.

The treble is ours!

What a remarkable and incredible moment for Manchester City!
What a time to be a City Fan. Wow.

PART 14
Amazing Club Records

Highest appearance maker: Alan Oakes (680)

Club record goal-scorer: Sergio Aguero (260)

First club to win an English domestic treble: 2018/19 (plus 2018 FA Community/Charity Shield)

Most points in a season (2 for a win): 62 (Division Two, 1946/47)

Most points in a season (3 for a win): 100 (Premier League, 2017/18)

Most league goals in a season: 108 (Division Two, 1926/27: 42 games) and Division One (2001/02: 46 games)

Most goals in a season (all competitions): 169 (2018/19)

Most league goals by one player in a season: 38: Tommy Johnson (Division One, 1928/29)

Most wins in a row (all competitions) - English top-flight record: 21 (19 December 2020 - 2 March 2021)

Most league wins in a row: 18 (26 August – 27 December 2017)

Most Premier League wins in a row: 11 (equalling City's previous record in 2017 and Chelsea's of 2008)

Most home league wins in a row: 20 (5 March 2011 – 21 March 2012)

Most home wins in a row (all competitions): 20 (9 September 2017 – 4 March 2018)

Most away league wins in a row: 11 (21 May 2017 - 27 December 2017)

Most away wins in a row (all competitions): 19 (19 December 2020 - 1 May 2021)

Club record unbeaten run: 28 (27 April 2017 - 3 December 2017 and 25 November 2020 - 2 March 2021)

Club record unbeaten run away from home: 22 (5 November 2020 - 1 May 2021)

Premier League record for the longest winning run of games in a calendar year: 13 (3 January - 2 March 2021)

Highest number of wins achieved in a single month in English football: 9: January 2021

Longest winning run by an English side in the Champions League: 7 (9 December 2020 - 4 May 2021)

Club record unbeaten home run in the Champions League: 14 (7 November 2018 - 4 May 2021)

Club record unbeaten run in the Champions League: 12 (21 October 2020 - 4 May 2021)

Most clean sheets in one season: 33 (61 matches, 2018/19)

Most clean sheets by an individual goalkeeper in one season: 29: Joe Hart (2010/11)

Most consecutive league clean sheets during a season: 6 (15 September 2018 – 29 October 2018)

Record league victory: 11–3 v Lincoln City, 23 March 1895

Record FA Cup victory: 12–0 v Liverpool Stanley, 4 October 1890

Record European victory: 7–0 v Schalke 04 (UEFA Champions League: Round of 16 second leg), 12 March 2019

Highest home attendance: 84,569 v Stoke City, 3 March 1934. (Record home attendance in English football)

Most capped player: David Silva (Spain)

PART 15

Manchester City Records and Historical Milestones

Records:

Record FA Cup victory: 12–0 v Liverpool Stanley, 4 October 1890

Record league victory: 11–3 v Lincoln City, 23 March 1895

Highest home attendance: 84,569 v Stoke City, 3 March 1934 (Record home attendance in English football)

Most points in a season (2 for a win): 62 (Division Two, 1946/47)

Most consecutive league clean sheets during a season: 6 (15 September 2018 – 29 October 2018)

Most clean sheets by an individual goalkeeper in one season: 29: Joe Hart (2010/11)

Most clean sheets in one season: 33 (61 matches, 2018/19)

Club record goal-scorer: Sergio Aguero (260)

Most goals in a season (all competitions): 169 (2018/19)

Most league goals in a season: 108 (Division Two, 1926/27: 42 games) and Division One (2001/02: 46 games)

Most goals by one player in a season: 38: Tommy Johnson (Division One, 1928/29)

First club to win an English domestic treble: 2018/19 (plus 2018 FA Community/Charity Shield)

Most points in a season (3 for a win): 100 (Premier League, 2017/18)

Most wins in a row (all competitions) - English top-flight record: 21 (19 December 2020 - 2 March 2021)

Most league wins in a row: 18 (26 August – 27 December 2017)

Most Premier League wins in a row: 11 (equalling City's previous record in 2017 and Chelsea's in 2008)

Most home league wins in a row: 20 (5 March 2011 – 21 March 2012)

Most home wins in a row (all competitions): 20 (9 September 2017 – 4 March 2018)

Most away league wins in a row: 11 (21 May 2017 - 27 December 2017)

Most away wins in a row (all competitions): 19 (19 December 2020 - 1 May 2021)

Club record unbeaten run: 28 (27 April 2017 - 3 December 2017 and 25 November 2020 - 2 March 2021)

Club record unbeaten run away from home: 22 (5 November 2020 - 1 May 2021)

Premier League record for the longest winning run of games in a calendar year: 13 (3 January - 2 March 2021)

Longest winning run by an English side in the Champions League: 7 (9 December 2020 - 4 May 2021)

Club record unbeaten home run in the Champions League: 14 (7 November 2018 - 4 May 2021)

Club record unbeaten run in the Champions League: 12 (21 October 2020 - 4 May 2021)

Most consecutive league clean sheets during a season: 6 (15 September 2018 – 29 October 2018)

Highest appearance maker: Alan Oakes (680)

Most capped player: David Silva (Spain)

Highest number of wins achieved in a single month in English football: 9: January 2021

Record European victory: 7–0 v Schalke 04 (UEFA Champions League: Round of 16 second leg), 12 March 2019

Historical Milestones

1994: The Kippax Stand is closed due to legislation, marking a significant moment in Manchester City's history.

1995/96: City experiences a tumultuous season, appointing three different managers, fueling intrigue and uncertainty.

1997: A new club badge is unveiled, a momentous occasion that adds a fresh chapter to City's visual identity.

1999: City achieves promotion through a penalty shoot-out victory in the Division Two Play-Off, epitomizing triumph amid nail-biting drama.

2000: City returns to the Premiership after back-to-back promotions, a testament to their resilience and determination.

2002: Stuart Pearce captains City during their promotion back to the Premiership, adding a personal touch to their triumphant return.

2003: An emotional farewell to Maine Road marks a poignant transition as City moves to the City of Manchester Stadium, heralding a new era.

2007: Sven Goran Eriksson takes the helm as manager, injecting renewed hope and ambition into the club's trajectory.

2008: The Abu Dhabi United Group becomes the new owners of Manchester City, revolutionizing the club's fortunes, while Robinho's acquisition with a British transfer record fee ignites a wave of anticipation.

2009: Roberto Mancini takes the managerial reins, inspiring a new era of tactical brilliance and strategic vision.

2010: City enjoys their best-ever Premier League campaign and reaches the League Cup semi-finals, a season adorned with moments of sheer brilliance.

2011: City secures the FA Cup and Champions League qualification, signaling their ascent to the pinnacle of English football.

2012: City clinches the Premier League championship, ending a 44-year wait for domestic glory, amid jubilant celebrations.

2014: City captures the Capital One Cup and the Premier League title, reaffirming their dominance on the domestic front.

2016: City adds another League Cup triumph to their cabinet, etching their name as a force to be reckoned with in cup competitions.

2018: City secures the Carabao Cup and the Premier League crown for the fifth time, etching their name in history as serial champions.

2019: A triumphant season sees City claim the Carabao Cup, Premier League, and FA Cup, completing a domestic treble for the first time.

2020: City secures a third-successive League Cup, continuing their relentless pursuit of silverware.

2021: City secures their third Premier League title in four seasons, accompanied by a fourth successive League Cup triumph, solidifying their status as a footballing powerhouse.

2022 - 2023: City claims a fourth Premier League title in five years, a testament to their sustained excellence and dominance in English football.

PART 16

And Finally

In the grand tapestry of Manchester City's future, a symphony of anticipation and intrigue weaves its mesmerizing melody. Like shooting stars in the vast expanse, the limitless possibilities beckon, promising a brilliance that defies the imagination. Will the blue moon rise, casting a radiant glow on a path paved with unyielding triumph? A constellation of new heroes, adorned in sky blue, may etch their names into the hallowed halls of football's pantheon. The enigma of what awaits Manchester City lies in the hands of time, its secrets shrouded in mystery.

Amidst the ever-changing landscape, Manchester City stands poised to script their destiny. With unwavering resolve, they march forward, hungering for glory's embrace. The future canvas is blank, awaiting the brushstrokes of ingenuity and tactical brilliance. With the world as a witness, the question echoes: What heights will Manchester City scale next? The journey promises an exhilarating rollercoaster, daring challenges, and moments that will reverberate in the hearts of fans for eternity.

Yet, amidst the unpredictable, one thing is constant: Manchester City's unwavering identity. Rooted in heritage, fueled by visionary leadership, they embrace a philosophy that transcends the pitch. The beautiful game courses through their veins, a dedication to attacking football and a nurturing embrace of academy talent. As generations pass the baton, the essence of Manchester City stands resolute. The future cradles the promise of further refinement, igniting global passion and leaving an indelible legacy.

So, let us embark on this voyage of uncertainty, brimming with fervor and anticipation. The future of Manchester City stands as an untamed enigma, its secrets yearning to be unveiled. Each step, each touch of the ball, weaves a spellbinding tale, a narrative that will seize our hearts and mold the destiny of this extraordinary club. The riddle of Manchester City's future unravels with the passage of time, as the world watches in awe, eager for the unfolding of their next legendary chapter.

Disclaimer

Although every effort has been made to assure the correctness and integrity of the information in this book, it is nevertheless conceivable that some historical references may be inaccurate. All of the references in this book have undergone thorough and sincere study.

Printed in Great Britain
by Amazon

35380219R00071